America's Deadliest Shipwrecks: The History of the SS *Sultana*, the SS *Eastland*, and the PS *General Slocum*

By Charles River Editors

The Sultana near Helena, Arkansas in April 1865

About Charles River Editors

Charles River Editors provides superior editing and original writing services across the digital publishing industry, with the expertise to create digital content for publishers across a vast range of subject matter. In addition to providing original digital content for third party publishers, we also republish civilization's greatest literary works, bringing them to new generations of readers via ebooks.

Sign up here to receive updates about free books as we publish them, and visit Our Kindle Author Page to browse today's free promotions and our most recently published Kindle titles.

Introduction

The Explosion of the SS Sultana (1865)

A 19th century illustration of the Sultana on fire

There is a popular saying that declares "timing is everything," and in no other field of study is that truer than in history. For instance, under normal conditions, a ship that sank with more than 2,000 passengers aboard – most of whom died – would be big news, yet today the sinking of the SS *Sultana* is often overlooked if not entirely forgotten. While it might have generated the type of publicity and reaction of the Johnstown Flood of 1889 or the Galveston Hurricane of 1900 under normal circumstances, the explosion and sinking of the *Sultana* on April 27, 1865 has become something of a historical footnote.

The irony is that the *Sultana* is a historical footnote because of the Civil War, but it was also intimately tied to the war. Although Robert E. Lee's surrender to Ulysses Grant at Appomattox was not technically the end of the Civil War, it took one of the last remaining Confederate armies out of the field. Furthermore, on the night of April 14, many of the Union's hopes for the future were dashed when President Abraham Lincoln was shot at Ford's Theatre in Washington, D. C. The people of the nation quickly became a volatile mix of grief and outrage, uninterested in anything that did not relate to the death of their beloved president. In fact, just the day before the disaster, as the Sultana was sailing up the Mississippi River to her rendezvous with destiny,

Union Army soldiers cornered and killed Lincoln's assassin, John Wilkes Booth. The Sultana's chief engineer, N. Wintringer, tried to give his readers a sense of the context in which the accident took place when he wrote, "As I was chief engineer of that ill-fated steamer at the time of her explosion I thought that my recollections of that terrible calamity would be of some interest. I believe that George Oayton, one of the pilots and myself were the only officers of the boat that escaped with our lives. ... The 'Sultana' left Cairo on that fatal trip the 15th of April, 1865, the day after the death of President Lincoln, and as all wire communications with the south were cut off at that time, the 'Sultana' carried the news of his assassination and death to all points and military posts on the Mississippi river as far as New Orleans." In short, the entire nation was in a state of chaos and too exhausted from four years of war that culminated in the death of the president to give the disaster the attention and grief it deserved.

Perhaps the cruelest irony of the disaster is that the *Sultana* was packed full of men who had survived every conceivable trial and tribulation of the war, from wounds and sicknesses to being prisoners. Having lost hundreds of thousands, America was almost numb to the loss of a couple of thousand more, especially when many of the dead were soldiers themselves, and in a sense, it was left for future generations to try to unravel what went wrong and to pay tribute to the men who died on that dark night.

America's Deadliest Shipwrecks: The History of the SS Sultana, the SS Eastland, and the PS General Slocum chronicles the story of America's deadliest maritime disaster. Along with pictures of important people, places, and events, you will learn about the explosion and sinking of the Sultana like never before, in no time at all.

The PS *General Slocum*

The Sinking of the General Slocum (June 15, 1904)

"There were scenes of horror on the General Slocum and on shore such as it would not be decent to set down on paper..." – J.S. Ogilvie, *History of the General Slocum disaster by which nearly 1200 lives were lost by the burning of the steamer General Slocum in Hell gate, New York harbor, June 15, 1904* (1904)

There is a popular saying that declares "timing is everything," and in no other field of study is that truer than in history. For instance, under normal conditions, a ship that sank with more than 1,000 passengers aboard – most of whom died – would be big news, yet today the sinking of the PS *General Slocum* is often overlooked if not entirely forgotten. While it might have generated the type of publicity and reaction of the Johnstown Flood of 1889 or the Galveston Hurricane of 1900 under normal circumstances, deadliest disaster in New York City's history before 9/11, and the second deadliest maritime disaster in peacetime in American history has become something of a historical footnote.

On June 15, 1904, an annual gala was held on the passenger ship as it steamed up the East River, with about 1,400 people from St. Mark's Evangelical Lutheran Church. Consisting mostly of German immigrants, the boat was packed with women and children, and when a small fire started on the ship shortly after the trip began, faulty equipment was unable to put it out or stop it from spreading. On top of that, the lifeboats were tied up and the crew, which never conducted emergency drills, was unprepared for a potential disaster. When parents put life preservers on their children and then had them enter the water, they soon learned that the life preservers were also faulty and didn't float.

As the disaster unfolded, over 1,000 passengers burned to death or drowned, many swept under the water by the East River's current and weighed down by heavy wool clothing. Few people on board knew how to swim, exacerbating the situation, and eventually the overcrowded decks began to collapse, crushing some unfortunate victims.

In the end, the *General Slocum* sank in shallow water while hundreds of corpses drifted ashore, and the fallout was immediate. The captain was indicted for criminal negligence and manslaughter, and the ship's owner was also charged. While the captain would receive a 10 year sentence, the company in charge of the *General Slocum* got off with a light fine. In a somewhat fitting postscript, the ship was salvaged and converted into a barge, only to sink once again during a heavy storm in 1911.

It is said that time heals all wounds, but in the case of the *Slocum* disaster, the wounds weren't so much healed as overshadowed. The Triangle Shirtwaist Factory fire took over 100 lives in New York City in 1911 and led to calls for serious workplace reforms, and a few years later, World War I began in Europe. With that, much of the sympathy Americans previously felt for the loss of over 1,000 German lives on the *Slocum* evaporated.

America's Deadliest Shipwrecks: The History of the SS Sultana, the SS Eastland, and the PS General Slocum chronicles the fateful chain of events that led to one of the worst tragedies in American history. Along with pictures of important people, places, and events, you will learn about the *General Slocum* like never before, in no time at all.

The SS *Eastland* Disaster (July 24, 1915)

A picture of the *Eastland* on its side in the Chicago River

"And then movement caught my eye. I looked across the river. As I watched in disoriented stupefaction a steamer large as an ocean liner slowly turned over on its side as though it were a whale going to take a nap. I didn't believe a huge steamer had done this before my eyes, lashed to a dock, in perfectly calm water, in excellent weather, with no explosion, no fire, nothing. I thought I had gone crazy." – Jack Woodford, writer

The Great Lakes have claimed countless thousands of vessels over the course of history, including swallowing up gigantic freighters like the *Edmund Fitzgerald*, the largest ship of its day to sail the Great Lakes and still the largest to lie below Lake Superior's murky depths. Given the dangerous conditions and precarious history associated with America's largest freshwater lakes, it's somewhat ironic that the deadliest maritime disaster took place in Chicago aboard a ship that capsized while docked to a pier.

When people discuss deadly maritime disasters during the second decade of the 20th century in which more than 800 people were killed, they're often talking about the Titanic or Lusitania, not the Eastland on the Chicago River. However, shockingly enough, on July 24, 1915, a ship full of sightseers out for a day on the Great Lakes capsized while still tied to a dock, sending more than 2,500 passengers into the frigid water. By the time the ship was righted and rescue efforts were completed, nearly 850 people had been killed.

As unbelievable as the incident seemed, the *Eastland* was actually susceptible to just such a problem as a result of its issues with listing, and on top of that, the ship seemed to have all sorts of bad luck in its past, including a collision with another boat and even a mutiny on board. If anything, the safety protocols established after the sinking of the Titanic, most notably the inclusion of enough lifeboats on board for every passenger, made the *Eastland* even more top heavy and contributed to the disaster. Ultimately, several individuals were charged with crimes in connection with the *Eastland* disaster, but none would be found guilty.

America's Deadliest Shipwrecks: The History of the SS Sultana, the SS Eastland, and the PS General Slocum chronicles the story of the disaster and its aftermath. Along with pictures of important people, places, and events, you will learn about the *Eastland* like never before, in no time at all.

The SS *Sultana*

Chapter 1: Sultana Sounds Her Farewell Blast

"Midnight's dreary hour has past,

The mists of night are falling fast.

Sultana sounds her farewell blast.

And braves the mighty stream;

The swollen river's banks o'erflow.

The leaden clouds are hanging low

And veil the stars' bright silver glow.

And darkness reigns supreme." – William H. Norton, "The Burning of the Sultana"

The *Sultana*

One of the many ironies of the sinking of the Sultana was that the men that it killed were supposed to finally be safe. After surviving up to four years of combat, injury, sickness and near starvation, they were going home. Many of them had not seen their families since the spring of 1861, and even more of them had spent most of the last year in an underfunded Confederate prison. Because of Union blockades, the Confederate army and civilian populations were starving, and since they also had almost no medical supplies left for their own sick and injured, Union prisoners were an afterthought. After all, with little to no food for their own families, they had even less to share with their captured enemies. As a result, Confederate prisoner of war camps were among the worst in 19th century history.

One can appreciate, then, Chester Berry's sense of a mix of relief and concern when he heard that the war might be over: "From Meridian we were taken to Jackson, Miss., then marched across the country to the Big Black River, crossing it on the 1st day of April, 1865, lacking one day of ten months that I had been in the hands of the confederate authorities — and I could not say yet that I was out of their hands, for we were put into a camp called 'Camp Fisk,' which is four miles from Vicksburg, and were under a confederate major, but fed, clothed, and sheltered by "Uncle Samuel."

Berry went on to explain that with the war drawing to a close, the Confederacy had asked the Union Army for supplies to feed and care for the prisoners in their charge until they could be discharged. The result was something of an unusual arrangement, possible only within the context of a civil war between brothers: "We understood at the time, and I do still, that our government had made a proposition to the confederate authorities that if they would remove their prisoners on to neutral ground, they might still have control of them, but our government would feed, clothe and shelter us. I never experienced a happier day in my life than I did when we marched under the old Stars and Stripes at the Big Black River railroad bridge and drew my first cup of coffee and a single hard tack. It looked like a stingy way for "Uncle Sam" to do business, but the boys who served us told us that when the first squad of prisoners arrived that they (the cooks) kicked open the boxes of hard-tack among them, just as they had been in the habit of doing among themselves, and the result was that there was a number of deaths before night; so we were happy with our meager rations, finding more joy in looking up at the old flag..."

Otto Barden was one of those who was trying to process all that had happened. He also described the circumstances and emotions surrounding his release: "The rebels sent us to Vicksburg, where we remained in parole camp. While here we heard of the sad news of the assassination of President Lincoln by a rebel. The prisoners became wild with indignation and started for the rebel head-quarters. The rebel major that had charge of us fled across the Big Black River Bridge for safety until we learned the particulars of the President's death. We were put on the steamer, "Sultana." About 2,400 men were on their way to "God's country," as we called the North, and we all felt happy to know that we were on our way home and that the war was over (Hallelujah. Amen)"

Now that the war was over, it was time to head home. The men were released from their prison camp and turned over to their own officers, who were to arrange for them to get back to their homes. That is where the trouble began. By the time the Sultana arrived from Illinois to take its share of men north to their homes, there were nearly 5,000 newly released prisoners packed into the former Confederate stronghold, Camp Fisk, outside of Vicksburg, Tennessee. While they finally had their freedom and plenty to eat, they did not have proper shelter and were forced to construct what small shelters they could against the elements.

Not surprisingly, the Union generals were anxious to get these men off their hands and back to their homes. As is so often the case in war or any other situation, savvy businessmen were just as anxious to help them, for a price. Berry later reported the rumors swirling around the dock that day: "I understood at the time, and have had no reason to change my mind, that it was a contrived plan with the United States' quartermaster at Vicksburg and the captain of the boat. ... The officers of the steamers, knowing that the men would pay almost any price, charged exorbitant rates of fare to Cairo, Illinois. ...General Grant learned what had been done. He at once sent an officer to tie up the boats and ordered that all but $5 from each private and $10 from each commissioned officer be refunded. The government adopted that rule, and whenever troops were sent by private boats they were allowed $5 per man for transportation. There were a number of boats at Vicksburg at the time we were to be sent north, but all demanded the $5 per man and would take but 1,000 men. Finally the quartermaster succeeded in persuading the captain of the 'Sultana' to take the entire 2,000 at 13 per head, that would give him $6,000 for the trip, whereas if he only took 1,000 at $5 he would only make $5,000. The report said that the captain of the 'Sultana' signed the papers for $10,000, and that the quartermaster cashed them on the spot for $6,000."

Chapter 2: As Sultana Steams in the Dead of Night

"Her engine fires now brighter burn,

Her mammoth wheels now faster turn.

Her dipping paddles lightly spurn

The river's foaming crest;

And drowsy Memphis, lost to sight,

Now fainter shows her beacon light,

As Sultana steams in the dead of night,

And the Union soldiers rest." - William H. Norton, "The Burning of the Sultana"

THE TRAGIC STEAMER SULTANA.

19th century depiction of the Sultana

And so it was that the captain of the Sultana, J. Cass Mason, joined a number of other captains of steamships in a quick journey south to see how they could line their own pockets while transporting the North's heroes back to their families. Since each man was worth the price of a steamboat ticket, he figured the more, the merrier.

Of course, that was in fact not true. As Brevet Brigadier General W. Hoffman explained following the accident, "The testimony shows that it was well understood by the four officers named that the troops in question were to embark on the 'Sultana.' ... Nothing was known positively as to the number of men that were to go on board, but it was the impression that there would be from 1,300 to 1,500; nor was any inspection of the boat made by either of the officers above named to determine her capacity or her condition. Neither one of them knew whether she had proper apparatus for cooking for so many men, or other necessary conveniences required for troops on transports."

The Sultana was designed to carry fewer than 400 passengers, but instead, she was crowded with as many as 2,400 men. Even worse, according to Hoffman, was the fact that those in charge knew there was a problem and did nothing to fix it. He noted, "As the men were being embarked Captain Kernes seems to have been satisfied that too many were going on one boat and he so reported to Colonel Hatch, who agreed with him in this belief but failed to interfere himself, as it was his duty to do, or to make any report of the matter to General Dana, because, as he states, he had had a day or two before some difficulty with Captain Speed about the shipment of troops.

There were two other steamers at the landing during the day, both of which would have taken a part of the men, and there was, therefore, no necessity for crowding them all on one boat ; it only required an order from Colonel Hatch, or a representation of the facts to the commanding general."

This led Hoffman to the following scathing conclusion about how the disaster was unintentionally orchestrated by the very officers sworn to lead those in their charge: "Upon a careful consideration of all the facts as presented in the testimony herewith submitted, I am of the opinion that the shipment of so large a number of troops on one boat, was, under the circumstances, unnecessary, unjustifiable, and a great outrage on the troops. A proper order was issued by the general commanding the department for the embarkation of the paroled prisoners, and there were four officers of his staff who were responsible that this order was properly carried out... If there was anything deficient or unsuitable in the character of the transportation furnished, one or more of these officers should be held accountable for the neglect."

Sadly, this was not the first charge laid against Colonel Reuben Hatch, the officer in charge of transporting the prisoners home. He had a reputation for shady dealings in the past, and it seems, based on Hoffman's report, that he may very well have been the beneficiary of some sort of graft in this case. Just two month earlier, he had been judged "totally unfit" to continue in his office as quartermaster. However, instead of discharging him or pressuring him to resign, those above him sent him to Vicksburg, perhaps in a move designed to get him away from public notice.

To be fair, the soldiers were not at first inclined to complain about being crowded. They already had been through so much together that a few more days in close quarters was not going to bother anyone. Also, they were going home, and as anyone who has ever been stationed far from their family will admit, once the chance to get home arises, no one wants to delay it. As A.A. Jones recounted, "Here it was we wrote the happy news to our parents, wives, and sweethearts that we would soon be with them at home. How our hearts leaped within us with anticipation. On the morning of April 25th the news came that transportation had been secured, and we were marched out, with light hearts, to Vicksburg where the ^'Sultana" lay awaiting us. It was not at all necessary to be invited to go on board, and as we did so we noticed the repairing of the boilers ... The repairs of the boilers, the overcrowded condition of the boat, the drunken captain, who furnished transportation — made everything blue — because the captain of the boat objected to taking on so many. These very important things were unnoticed by the comrades in their anxiety to reach home and friends once more. But the sequel proves we should have been more wary. Near the bow of the hurricane deck was the place selected by our squad who had stuck together through all our afflictions during the war." The men trusted their officers and had been trained to obey orders, so if they were ordered onto a crowded ship, they would march onto a crowded ship.

That said, not every soldier on the Sultana had been a prisoner of war. Some of them, like

Daniel McLeod, had just been discharged from the army and were heading home. While he was just as happy as any of his comrades to be heading home, he later observed, "I was a passenger on the steamer 'Sultana,' en route from New Orleans to St. Louis. When the steamer reached Vicksburg one of the boilers was leaking and was patched by Klien's foundry men before the soldiers were put on board. There was no necessity of loading the " Sultana " so heavily, as the steamers 'Pauline Carroll' and 'Lady Gay' were at the landing coming up light, but the clerk and captain of the 'Sultana' were part owners of the boat, and I understood at the time that they put up money to get the transportation of the soldiers, which the officers of the other boats, having no interest, would not do."

While most of the passengers on the Sultana were soldiers, it is important to note that there were about 180 others on board, including private passengers and crewmen. Among these were several families with children, as well as 10 members of the Ladies Christian Commission. These passengers, along with the 2,000 soldiers loaded, brought the ship's numbers up to about 2,200 souls, more than five times what it was designed to carry.

Had the Sultana been a well-built vessel, all might have been well, even in spite of the overcrowded conditions. However, she was not, having been quickly constructed just two years earlier during the austerity of the war. Wintringer wrote, "While at Vicksburg we repaired a boiler. Now it was claimed by some at the time that this boiler was not properly repaired, and that was the cause of the explosion. In a short time those boilers were recovered and the one that had been repaired at Vicksburg was found in good condition, whole and intact, and that it was one of the other three that caused the explosion. Now what did cause this explosion? The explosion of the 'Walker R. Carter' and 'Missouri,' in rapid succession, I think fully answers that question. It was the manner of the construction of those boilers. After these three fatal explosions they were taken out of all steamers using them and replaced with the old style of boiler. They were an experiment on the lower Mississippi. They had been used with some success on the upper Mississippi, where the water at all times is clear and not liable to make much sediment or scale. As I said before, those boilers were an experiment on the lower Mississippi, and had not long been in use there, and it was the opinion of experts that it would have been only a question of time for all steamers using those boilers to have gone the way that the 'Carter,' 'Missouri,' and 'Sultana' went, had they not have been taken out and replaced by others."

It seems that the Sultana had already been experiencing trouble with her boilers before she ever docked in Vicksburg. According to Henry J. Lyda, "I was employed on board the steamer 'Sultana,' but left the boat about two hours before it left St. Louis for New Orleans on her fatal trip. In my estimation it was carelessness on the part of the captain and engineer that caused the disaster. The '* Sultana's" boilers were not fit for duty, as that steamer stopped at Natchez and Vicksburg on the last two trips before the explosion to patch and repair her boilers. She had the tubular boilers which have been done away with since that time."

Chapter 3: The Sleeping Soldiers Dream of Home

"The sleeping soldiers dream of home.

To them the long sought day had come.

No more in prison pens to moan,

Or guarded by the gray;

At last the changing fates of war

Had swung their prison 'gates ajar,'

And "laurel wreaths" from the North afar

Await their crowning day." - William H. Norton, "The Burning of the Sultana"

The engines that were designed to propel the weight of the ship and about 400 people was being forced to carry an additional 20,000 pounds of human cargo upstream and against the strong current of the mighty Mississippi. The perfect stage had been set for disaster, and some people were worried about it. William Boor, of Pennsylvania, was concerned with the safety of the boilers, and it saved his life, as well as the lives of some of his friends. He explained, "When going on board my attention was attracted by the noise and work at the boilers going on at that time. We were marched to the hurricane deck and informed that this was to be our place of abode, but I thought different. I turned to Comrade Wm. A Hulit, and, asking him to take charge of our clothing which I had at the time, I went below and looked at the boilers, which were not very favorable to my mind. I went back to the boys, told them that we had better look for some other place and that I thought that there was danger; and if the boat should blow up and we were on that deck we would go higher than a kite. We started for the deck below, taking our position at the head of the stairway."

Unfortunately, most of the other soldiers were too weakened by their prison stays and dazzled by their sudden release to pay attention to their surroundings. As Walter Elliott put it, "On our arrival at prison camp, six miles in rear of Vicksburg, we received a glorious welcome and invitation to "take something;" that is, we were taken to the Commissary, where barrel after barrel of pickled cabbage was rolled out and the heads knocked in, and we, marching round and round, gobbled out and ravenously devoured the cabbage and licked the vinegar from our fingers, the sweetest dainty to my bleeding gums that ever I tasted. We feasted on pickles. Next day we exchanged our filthy rags for clean clothing, wrote home, rested and feasted. About 2,500 embarked on the Sultana for St Louis, together with a good many passengers, crowded, jammed and packed on all the decks and guards and in the cabin. But what cared the survivors of Andersonville — the war was over and we were going home."

The boat finally was loaded to its rafters by midnight on the April 25th and set sail at about 1:00 a.m. on the 26th. The men were in good spirits and had enough to eat, though not by much, as the ship's kitchens were terribly overworked trying to provide for them. They sailed on up the Mississippi all day on the 26th until they reached their next destination. As Elliott wrote, "Nothing unusual occurred until we reached Memphis, although I had suffered much from fear of the boys crowding to one side of the boat and capsizing her. One instance in particular: While at Helena a photographer was 'taking' the boat, and each soldier seemed to be bent on having his face discernible in the picture. I entreated and exhorted prudence, while I sat on the roof, my feet pendant and my hands on a float, momentarily expecting a capsizing and sinking."

The Helena picture

Photography still was in its infancy at this time, but war-related subjects were popular. No doubt the man taking the picture thought it a way to commemorate the Union victory and the return of peace. After all, what could be more heartening than a photograph of a thousand or more paroled solders going home? Ironically, this photo would later be used as pictorial evidence for just how overcrowded the ship was. It would be studied by grieving families for years, as each sought to catch one final glimpse of a loved one just hours before his death.

By the evening of the 26th, the men were beginning to grow uncomfortable in their crowded spaces. James Brady remembered, "Our condition on this boat was more like a lot of hogs than men. With the other passengers and crew, there were about 2,100 in all, besides a freight cargo, making in all more than double the carrying capacity of the boat. We were headed up the river for Cairo, 111. The boat landed at Memphis, Tenn., on the evening of April 26, where a part of the freight as unloaded. Some time after we steamed up the river, making a landing to take on coal. My friend, David Ettleman, and I went up to the hurricane deck and made our bed, as we were crowded too much below, and laid down."

While his passengers were trying to find a few feet of deck space on which to lay down for the night, Captain Mason had overseen the unloading of his cargo in Memphis and turned the ship over to a lesser officer for the night. It may have been at around this time that he began to regret overloading his boat. According to William Fies, "The 'Sultana' landed at Memphis, Tennessee, on the evening of April 26, where a portion of her cargo of freight was discharged. Sometime during that night the boat left the wharf at Memphis and steamed up the river, making a landing to take on coal. Before we left Memphis my bunk-mate, comrade A. 0. Oranmer, of my company, and I fixed down our bed on the cabin deck and on the starboard side near the railing. I remember, just before I fell asleep, Captain Mason, in command of the boat, came up from below, to go to his stateroom I presume, and was compelled to crawl around on the rail, as the deck was so crowded with men lying down that he could not find room to step, and was in consequence made the subject of several jokes."

Chapter 4: And Mothers Wear Their Wonted Smile

"For Peace has raised her magic hand,

The Stars and Stripes wave o'er the land,

The conquered foemen now disband,

'As melts the morning dew;'

And mothers wear their wonted smile,

And aged sires the hours beguile.

And plighted love awaits the while

The coming of the blue." - William H. Norton, "The Burning of the Sultana"

Once they were on the ship and freed from their prisons, the soldiers believed that the threat of death was behind them, not approaching. Elliott, for one, was more interested in the present and future than the past: "Each night the cabin was filled with a row of double deck cots. I had been fortunate in securing one of these, but on the night previous to reaching Memphis, I suddenly conceived and executed the purpose of making a stranger, whose name I never knew — our Commissary Sergeant in parole camp — occupy my cot while I spent the night in a chair. The boat lay at the Memphis wharf discharging freight, and the cots were being placed, when my friend of the night before came to me and asked if I had a cot. I pointed to my hat, placed on one to hold it. He said that one was in a hot, unpleasant and dangerous place over the boilers, and that he had reserved one for me in the ladies' cabin; that I had my way the night before, and he must have his way now. 'Give it to some poor fellow who had none last night,' I said; but a moment afterwards he came and told me he had removed my hat to the cot selected by him, and that I would have to take that or none. Soon I retired to the cot, read until weary, fell asleep, was partly aroused by the boat leaving the wharf a little after midnight, but relapsed into sweet slumber, dreaming of the loved ones at home — a motherless daughter, a noble Christian mother, two devoted sisters, and my brothers. How I reveled in the joy of the reunion."

Isaac Van Nuys also was thinking of his home and family: "Now, however, they were en route for home, the cruel war was over and their cause triumphant. The visions of loved ones greeting their return, and of dear familiar scenes and the quiet peaceful life were again theirs to pursue. All this filled their hearts with joy, making their bearing and conversation a study in human nature, rare even in those stirring days." Similarly, Chester Berry lulled himself to sleep thinking of home: "All went gay as a marriage bell for a while. A happier lot of men I think I never saw than those poor fellows were …The main thought that occupied every mind was home, the dearest spot on earth. I well remember, as the boat lay at Memphis unloading over one hundred hogsheads of sugar from her hold, that my thoughts not only wended northward, but I put them in practical shape. The Christian commission had given me a hymn book. At the time I left home the song 'Sweet Hour of Prayer' was having quite a run. I found this, and before the darkness had stopped me in the evening I had committed those words to memory and sang them for the boys, little dreaming how soon I should have to test the power of prayer as well as the hour when it was held."

Some of the men, such as George Anderson, took advantage of their time docked in Memphis to enjoy some "shore leave" and recalled, "When we arrived at Memphis, Tenn., two of my comrades and myself got off and went up into the city, and while there, I can assure you, I did not expect to be there in the morning. Got on board the steamer again; on the hurricane deck, near the pilot house, my two comrades and myself bunked for the night under one blanket."

Berry and some of the other men were talking, as people on a trip are wont to do, about what could go wrong. Little did they realize just how soon they'd regret their idle words. Berry later wrote, "There had been considerable talk among the boys, that it would be a grand opportunity for guerillas. If they only knew that there was such a boat-load of prisoners coming up the river, how they could plant a battery on the shore, sink the boat, and destroy nearly if not all of the prisoners on board; consequently, when the terrific explosion took place, and I was awakened from a sound sleep by a stick of cord wood striking me on the head and fracturing my skull, the first thought I had was that, while the boat lay at Memphis, someone had gone up the river and prepared such a reception for us, and what had only been a talk was now a realization."

Meanwhile, C.M. Nisley was watching the ship's maneuvers from the deck: "The steamer crossed the river to the coal barges and took on a supply of coal and, shortly after midnight or virtually on the morning of the 27th of April, started up the river again and had run about seven miles when the explosion took place."

Ben Davis may have been the last civilian to see the boilers working, but unfortunately, he was not able to shed any light on the disaster. He only was able to recall, "About two o'clock in the morning I got up to have a smoke. I went to the boilers to get a light for my pipe and going back to the hurricane deck, where I had been sleeping, I sat down for about ten minutes. When I got through with my smoke I got a canteen of water, and was about to take a drink when the boiler exploded and the canteen flew out of my hand."

Chapter 5: A Burst! A Crash! And Timbers Fly

"On sails the steamer through the gloom,

On sleep the soldiers to their doom,

And death's dark angel oh! So soon

Calls loud the muster roll.

A burst a crash and timbers fly,

And flame and steam leap to the sky,

And men awakened but to die

Commend to God their souls." - William H. Norton, "The Burning of the Sultana"

A 19th century depiction of the explosion

When the fatal explosion occurred aboard the *Sultana*, Berry knew something had gone terribly wrong, but he didn't yet know what it was. Shocked by what he'd just heard and seen, he froze. A moment later, he might have wished he had never moved on: "I lay low for a moment, when the hot water soaking through my blanket made me think I had better move. I sprang to the bow of the boat, and turning I looked back upon one of the most terrible scenes I ever beheld. The upper decks of the boat were a complete wreck, and the dry casings of the cabins falling in upon the hot bed of coal was burning like tinder. A few pails full of water would have put the fire out, but alas, it was ten feet to the water and there was no rope to draw with, consequently the flames swept fiercely up and back through the light wood of the upper decks. I had often read of burning vessels and nights of horror on the deep, and almost my first thought was, 'now, take in the scene,' but self-preservation stood out strongest."

To his credit, once Berry started moving, he quickly developed a plan of action. It is hard to say based on his personal recollection, but it seems that Berry had an excellent sense of self-preservation and a clear head in a time of crisis. While many of those around him were panicking, he took time to take stock of the situation and make a plan of escape: "I went back to where I had lain and found my bunk mate, Busley, scalded to death; I then secured a piece of cabin door casing, about three or four inches wide and about four feet long, then going back to the bow of the boat I came to the conclusion I did not want to take to the water just then, for it was literally black with human beings, many of whom were sinking and taking others with them. Being a good swimmer, and having board enough to save me, even if I were not, I concluded to wait till the rush was over."

At the time, others aboard the ship also were reacting to the crisis they were suddenly thrust into. What would soon become apparent is that one of the paddle wheeler's four boilers had exploded and, in turn, quickly caused two more to do the same. Otto Barden was one of the survivors closest to where the explosion occurred, and he described the scene: "On the morning of April 27, 1865, I was in the engine room of the steamer sound asleep, lying by the side of the hatch-hole with seven others of my regiment, when the explosion took place. First a terrific explosion, then hot steam, smoke, pieces of brick-bats and chunks of coal came thick and fast. I gasped for breath. A fire broke out that lighted up the whole river. I stood at this hatch-hole to keep comrades from falling in, for the top was blown off by the explosion. I stood here until the fire compelled me to leave. I helped several out of this place. I saw Jonas Huntsberger and John Baney go to the wheel-house, then I started in the same direction. I tried to get a large plank, but this was too heavy, so I left it and got a small board and started to the wheel to jump into the water. Here a young man said to me, 'you jump first, I cannot swim.' This man had all of his clothes on. I had just my shirt and pants on. I said to him, 'you must paddle your own canoe, I can't help you.' Then I jumped and stuck to my board."

Among those who were killed, the men closest to the explosion were the luckiest because they died instantly before even knowing what happened to them. On the other hand, while those slightly further away also were killed quickly, they died in agony as the superheated steam from the boilers scalded them so severely that they quickly passed out and died where they were. Others were killed by fire, a most dreadful death, trapped where they were.

Daniel Allen witnessed many people dying as he fought to save himself: "My escape and rescue from the ill-fated vessel were attended with much interest and excitement. The first I knew of the terrible disaster I was awakened, while in the stern of the lower deck, by the cry 'she's sinking,' and the shrieks and cries of the wounded and the terror stricken comrades. I pressed toward the bow, passing many wounded sufferers, who piteously begged to be thrown overboard. I saw men, while attempting to escape, pitch down through the hatchway that was full of blue curling flames, or rush wildly from the vessel to death and destruction in the turbid waters below. I clambered upon the hurricane deck and with calmness and self-possession assisted others to escape. At length, realizing that there was but little time to be lost, I divested myself of all clothing, and throwing a plank out, jumped into the water sixteen feet below."

Hiram Allison had just drifted off to sleep when he was very rudely awakened. He explained, "I was on the hurricane deck, close to the wheel house, lying down, and was just beginning to doze, when, all at once, I heard the crash. I jumped up the first thing, and saw a great hole torn through the hurricane deck and fire coming through. I stood a few minutes and looked at my surroundings. I concluded to take to the water. I climbed down from the hurricane deck to the cabin deck and took off all my clothes but my drawers and shirt, and then glanced round the burning wreck and saw that I would have to go, so I jumped from the cabin deck into the water."

Despite being hardened veterans of the nation's deadliest war, many of the survivors were unable to speak or even write about much of what they saw that night as the ship burned. Nonetheless, Chester Berry was able to recall and record at least one scene in excruciating detail:

> "After looking at the burning boat as long as I cared to, and as the waters were comparatively clear of men, I sprang overboard and struck out for some willows that I could see by the light of the burning boat, they appearing to be about one-half mile distant. I had gone but about twenty or thirty rods when, hearing a crash of breaking timbers, I looked back.
>
> The wheelhouse or covering for the wheel, (it was a side-wheel steamer,) had broken away partially from the hurricane deck, and a poor fellow had been in the act of stepping from the hurricane deck onto the wheel house. I presume it was then the hurricane deck fell in. When it reached an angle of about forty-five degrees it stopped, for some unaccountable reason, till it nearly burned up. He succeeded in reaching the wheel house but got no further, for it broke and let him part way through, then held him, as in an iron vice, till he burned to death, and even now, after the lapse of years, it almost seems as though I could hear the poor fellow's screams, as the forked flames swept around him."

During that evening that Berry saw a side of human behavior that few other people will ever see. He noted, "The horrors of that night will never be effaced from my memory — such swearing, praying, shouting and crying I had never heard ; and much of it from the same throat — imprecations followed by petitions to the Almighty, denunciations by bitter weeping." He would soon be surprised even by his own behavior.

James Brady also saw visions that would forever haunt him: "That was the last that I knew until the explosion, which occurred about two o'clock, A. m., at which time I was suddenly awakened to my senses, as the fire was all over me and my friend was trying to brush it off; it had already burned most of the hair off from the top of my head. We finally got the fire out and began looking around for some means of saving ourselves, for we could see that the boat was on fire. We could see nothing to get, so we went to the front end of the hurricane deck and took hold of some ropes and went down to the bow of the boat and Oh, what a sight met our gaze ! There were some killed in the explosion, lying in the bottom of the boat, being trampled upon, while some were crying and praying, many were cursing while others were singing. That sight I shall never forget; I often see it in my sleep, and wake with a start."

Chapter 6: Amid the Smoke and Fire and Glare

"Out from the flame's encircling fold,

Like a mighty rush of warriors bold.

They leap to the river dark and cold.

And search for the hidden shore.

In the cabins, and pinioned there,

Amid the smoke and fire and glare.

The awful wail of death's despair

Is heard above the roar." - William H. Norton, "The Burning of the Sultana"

Murry S. Baker was more fortunate than most of his comrades, as he at least faced the crisis on a full stomach. He explained, "I sat up till 12 o'clock, cooking rations, and then laid down and went to sleep. How long I had been sleeping I do not know. I was awakened by the explosion and sprang to my feet and looked around; someone said the boat was sinking; I went out on the stern and saw that it was not, and so went back. It was one of the worst sights I ever witnessed. Men who were scalded and bruised were crawling over one another to get out of the fire. I went to the side of the boat and pulled a board off to help me get ashore with, but a big 'Yank' grabbed it away from me. Then I got another off from a bunk and went down to the wheelhouse and threw it in the water, and then jumped after it."

At this time, the fight for survival became the most important matter on each living man's mind. Many acted nobly, discovering something deep inside themselves that they had not previously known existed. However, others acted on primal instinct, saying and doing things that they would never have done under normal circumstances. Chester Berry recorded such an incident: "I stood still and watched for a while, then began wandering around to other parts of the boat when I came across one man who was weeping bitterly and wringing his hands as if in terrible agony, continually crying, 'dear, dear.' I supposed the poor fellow was seriously hurt. My sympathies were aroused at once. Approaching him, I took him by the shoulder and asked where he was hurt. 'I'm not hurt at all,' he said, 'but I can't swim, I've got to drown, dear.' I bade him be quiet, then showing him my little board I said to him, 'there, do you see that; now you go to that pile of broken deck and get you one like it, and when you jump into the water put it under your chin and you can't drown.' 'But I did get one,' said he, 'and someone snatched it away from me.' 'Well then, get another,' said I. 'I did,' said he, ''and they took that away from me.' 'Well, then,' said I, 'get another.' 'Why,' said he, 'what would be the use, they would take it from me. Dear, I tell you there is no use; I've got to drown, I can't swim.' By this time I was thoroughly disgusted, and giving him a shove, I said, 'drown then you fool.'"

Berry's remark in the heat of that moment haunted him for the rest of his life, especially any time he had an occasion to remember the event. He wrote, "I want to say to you, gentle reader, I have been sorry all these years for that very act. There was little or no rush for the water at that time and had I given my board to that poor fellow, then conducted him to the edge of the boat and seen him safely overboard, he might, perhaps, have escaped, while, as it was, I have no doubt that he was drowned." It would be easy to judge him harshly for what he did, but it is only fair to remember that few will ever know the terror and panic he and the other men felt that night.

By this time, most of those who would survive the disaster were jumping or falling into the water to escape the burning hull of the Sultana. William Boor wrote of his attempts to rescue a friend, only to lose him in the end: "Comrade Thomas Brink was fastened in the wreck. I commenced clearing away the broken timbers that were about him and got him out. We went downstairs ; I asked him if he could swim, he said, 'yes, I can swim,' and I told him I could not swim, but would meet him somewhere on the shore. I was not, however, permitted to realize that happy event but was forced to the painful thought that he had perished, and the gallant Thomas Brink was no more."

Boor would have to wait until much later to mourn his friend, as would all the survivors. For the moment, they had to focus on navigating a path towards survival. Boor continued, "After I parted with my friend on the bow of the boat I went upstairs and got in under the wreck of the cabin roof. There I dressed, and took my rubber blanket and a spare shirt and tied them up, expecting if the board could carry me it also could carry my clothing, for I thought they would come good after having been in the icy cold water for a few hours. Now, I thought that I was prepared for any event that might overtake me. I went down on the boiler deck. While there I had a good view for quite a distance around the burning boat. It was a most distressing scene to see hundreds of men in the water pleading for help, clinching one another while they would hold on to each other — going down by the dozens at a time. At the same time I wonder how so many were saved as were, laboring under so many disadvantages, hundreds of them being thrown into the air as soon as the explosion took place, — scarcely having time to awake out of sleep, — and plunged into the water which was almost icy cold."

It soon became clear to Boor that the time for studying the situation was over: "The time for me to escape was now at hand for the fire was sweeping through the stairway. I had taken a survey of the river and made for the side which I thought was nearest the shore. Comrade Crawford of the 102d Regiment, and I started for the same place. At my saying to him we would have to leave he led the way, and I waited until the way was clear again." As it turned out, Boor almost waited too long, for "[w]hile waiting, my bundle caught fire, and, as I struck the water, I heard a hissing noise caused by the water coming in contact with the fire."

The loss of his clothes would soon prove to be the least of his worries: "Here I met with an accident which came near proving fatal to me. I got into one of those whirl-pools in the water, and while there I could not manage my board. I finally got tired out, and then for the first time I thought I must give up the struggle and drown as I could not get away from there. I finally concluded to dive to the bottom and get a good start not thinking that the water was forty or fifty feet deep in the channel. I went down but it was not long before I was in need of the fresh air.

When I came near the surface of the water, as luck would have it, I cleared the pool and got my board."

Chief engineer Wintringer was one of the last men off the sinking craft and had a bird's eye view of all the chaos around him. He wrote, "I stood bewildered for a moment, and then saw the river perfectly alive with human beings struggling in the water, and the cry from all quarters was "put out the fire," which was getting good headway by this time. But there was such a mass of confusion and such a complete wreck of the boat that nobody, apparently, could get out of the position they were in. I managed to get hold of a shutter and saw that the fire would soon force me off of the boat; I took my chances and jumped into the river."

Hosea Aldrich also bore witness to the chaos and was one of the few to notice what was happening to the non-military passengers aboard the ship. Like Boor, he was determined to try to get off the ship with at least a few of the belongings he had with him: "When it happened I was sound asleep, and the first thing that I knew or heard was a terrible crash, everything seemed to be falling. The things I had under my head, my shoes, and some other articles and specimens that I had gathered up and had them tied up in an old pair of drawers, they all went down through the floor. We scrambled back. The smoke came rushing up through the passage made by the exit of the exploded boiler. The cry from all was, 'What is the matter?' and the reply came, 'the boat is on fire.' It was all confusion. The screams of women and children mingled with the groans of the wounded and dying. Brave men rushed to and fro in the agony of fear, some uttering the most profane language and others commending their spirits to the Great Ruler of the Universe; the cries of the drowning and the roaring of the flames as they leaped heavenward made the scene most affecting and touching. But it was of short duration as the glare that illuminated the sky and made visible the awful despair of the hour soon died away while darkness more intense than ever settled down on the floating hulk and the victims of the disaster."

Chapter 7: They Battle With the Waves

"Out on the river's rolling tide,

Out from the steamer's burning side.

Out where the circle is growing wide.

They battle with the waves.

And drowning men each other clasp.

And witling in death's closing grasp

They struggle bravely, but at last

Sink to watery graves." - William H. Norton, "The Burning of the Sultana"

Otto Barden quickly learned that the water did not offer instant salvation from death. He wrote of his jump into the Mississippi, "I went down so far that I let go of my board and paddled to get on top of the water. I strangled twice before I reached the top; then the young man caught me and he strangled me twice. By this time I was about played out. I then reached the wheel, and clung to it until I tore off all of my clothes, with the intention of swimming with one hand."

The sight of a friendly face gave Barden the encouragement he needed to go on: "I looked around and recognized Fritz Saunders, of Ray Regiment, by my side. I said, 'Saunders, here is a door under the wheel, let us get it out.' We got it out and found it had glass panels in it. I said, 'let this go, here is a whole door.' The rest on the wheel took the first door and we started after them with the other. We had not more than started when a man swam up and laid across the center of our door. I looked back and saw the wheel-house fall — it had burned off and fell over. If we had remained there one minute longer it would have buried us in the fire. I said to Saunders, 'let's go to the right, it is nearer to shore.' He replied, 'no, there is a boat; I will paddle for it.' And when we were in the center of the river the steamer was about out of sight."

Based on the testimony of a number of survivors, it seems there was indeed another ship in the vicinity of the wreck that night, but it apparently didn't see the explosion because it kept on steaming along its course. There was, of course, no such thing as radio with which to contact the other vessel, so the men were left to fend for themselves. Barden continued, "We met three young men clinging to a large trunk; they grasped our door for us to steer them into the timber. We had not gone far until these bore too much weight on our door; that put us all under the water. I gave the trunk a kick and raised on the door and brought it to the surface of the water. Then I said, 'boys if you don't keep your weight off of the door, then you must steer the trunk yourselves. By this time I was cold and benumbed and was in a sinking condition, but having presence of mind I reached and got my board and called aloud to God for help. I rubbed my arms and got the blood in circulation again."

Fortunately, the Mississippi River, though wide, is a river and not an ocean or lake, so many of the men were able to make it to shore, though the shore was often overgrown and therefore offered only some relief to their experience in the water. Furthermore, there were small islands on the river, including one that Barden and many others made their way to. However, as he noted, being out of the water by no means meant being out of the cold: "Soon we were among the timber on the 'Hen and Chickens' island, clinging to trees, but being too cold and benumbed to climb a tree. I had the good luck of finding saplings under the water. I put my foot in the fork and raised myself out of the water. I soon got warm and swam to a larger tree, and clung to it, but was not there very long until I got so cold that I fell from the tree into the water. I swam to the same tree and clung to it and called aloud to God for His assistance. I saw a man break open this trunk, it contained only ladies' dresses so it was no help to us. One of these men that had clung to the trunk was so cold that he drowned with his arms around a tree. We were on these trees until about nine o'clock A.M. It seemed as if the gnats and mosquitoes would eat us alive."

While some men made it to shore, others continued their fight for survival, with some of them taking extreme measures to save their own lives. Some of them were subsequently haunted by their actions, like Chester Berry, but James Brady would not admit to any regrets about what he had done, at least not in writing: "After looking for something to save ourselves with in vain, we had about given ourselves up as lost, when all at once we saw a crowd with something which proved to be the gang plank. As this seemed to be our last chance my friend and I both grabbed hold of it, just as it was going over the side of the boat, and we all went down together. I think not less than forty or fifty men had hold of that plank, at least there were as many as could crowd around it when it went into the water, and it was very heavy. I ran beside it. It struck the water end first, and I thought it would never stop going down, but it finally did, and slowly arose to the surface. I think there were about fifteen or sixteen of us that had stuck to the plank. But now a new danger had seized me, as someone grabbed me by the right foot and it seemed as though it was in a vise; try as I would, I could not shake him off. I gripped the plank with all the strength that I had, and then I got my left foot between his hand and my foot and while holding on to the plank with both hands I pried him loose with my left foot, he taking my sock along with him, but he is welcome to the sock he sank out of sight and I saw him no more."

Brady's actions may sound harsh, but it is also not surprising given that the survivors were floating in near total darkness in very deep, muddy water. What light they had came only from their burning vessel. Furthermore, they were battle-hardened, having killed and risked being killed for the past several years, so any delicate sensibilities that they might have begun the war with had been thoroughly worn away. What was left behind made them what they really were: survivors.

Chester Berry was one of these survivors. By the time he was in the water, he already had done things he would never have thought himself capable of doing. Now all he had to do was live to tell the tale: "Just then I heard a glad cry from the burning boat and looking around discovered that past the boat, down the river, two or three miles as near as I could judge, was the bow light of a gun-boat. I turned and was now obliged to swim past the burning boat, for I was up the river about eighty rods above it; when nearly past the boat, which I kept a safe distance to my left, I ran into the top of a tree that had caved off from the bank and whose roots were now fast in the bed of the stream, upon which I climbed and was nearly asleep when a number of men from the boat came along and climbed upon it also."

Being dropped back into the freezing water he had just escaped ignited a new passion for survival in Berry's weary body, and a threat to what was then his most precious possession drove him into a form of madness: "Their united weight sank it low into the water, whose icy coldness coming upon my body again awakened me. Then, to more fully arouse me, a man got hold of my board and tried to take it away from me. I remonstrated with him, but he claimed the board belonged to him and that I was trying to steal it. This fully aroused me — it was the straw that broke the camel's back. Giving the board a quick jerk I sprang backward and went swimming down the stream on my back, holding my board high least I might lose it. I soon turned over and proceeded more slowly."

Unfortunately, the boost that adrenaline gave him soon wore off as hypothermia crept into his bones: "I began again to have an almost irresistible feeling of drowsiness. I was cold and sleepy." Fortunately, he came across a new form of salvation before his body gave in: "Just then I came across, or thought I did, a dry black ash sapling about two and one-half or three inches in diameter at the butt and six or eight feet long, that pronged in two branches about three feet from the butt end. I put this with my board and trying them found they would float. I then gave myself up to sleep and did not awake until long after sunrise. I then stood upon a large snag in the river that was pronged or forked something like I imagined the black ash sapling was in the night. I stood on the lower prong which was about a foot under water, while the upper prong was nearly two feet above the water, and, what to me was stranger than all, I had, instead of the little board four inches wide and about four feet long, a two inch plank about four inches wide and about six feet long."

Only later did Berry realize that what he experienced that night was hypothermia-induced hallucinations, or, as he put it, "I was out of my head and imagined that some terrible danger threatened me, but if I could only get that plank upon the upper prong of the snag, all would be safe. I soon came too enough to know that I was working a useless scheme; then I realized that it was worse than useless as it would take some of my strength to hold the plank on the snag while it would do me no good whatever."

With this realization, Berry nearly lost what was left of his mind, but by this time, the sun was up and he was beginning to come to his senses: "I then abandoned the project and began to cry with the pain of my fractured skull, but I soon stopped that also, saying to myself, crying does not ease pain. Then came the first clear thought of the morning and I realized what had happened and that I was but about five rods from the woods upon the Arkansas shore, the shore itself being under water."

Chapter 8: The Survivors of That Band

"Oh! For the star's bright silver light!

Oh! For a moon to dispel the night!

Oh! For the hand that should guide aright

The way to the distant land!

Clinging to driftwood and floating down,

Caught in the eddies and whirling around,

Washed to the flooded banks are found

The survivors of that band." - William H. Norton, "The Burning of the Sultana"

As Berry's account suggests, hypothermia would take as many lives as the explosion and fire did. Wintringer described how cold the water was, and the deadly effects it had on those trying to survive: "I was not in the water long until I came across a gangway plank about thirty feet long and fifteen inches wide. I abandoned my shutter for it. I was not there long until four others kept me company. There was just about enough buoyancy in the plank to keep our heads above water, and that was all. We floated in that manner for about two hours when we lodged against a snag, when one poor fellow became so benumbed with cold that he could hold no longer and sank to rise no more."

Many of those who were able to get out of the water found refuge in unusual vessels. Hiram Allison recalled, "I ... came across a horse trough with a comrade on each end of it. I took the center. When I caught up with the two comrades they were both praying. When I got on with them I said: 'That was a terrible disaster.' They made no reply but kept right on praying. I said no more to them and when it was light enough for me to see they were gone." Allison remained afloat in his horse trough until he was rescued.

The rescue of a number of men by an unexpected source testified to the fact that the war was well and truly over. As P.S. Atchley put it, "My experience on that terrible morning no pen can write nor tongue can tell. I was thrown into the surging waves of that mighty river, into the jaws of death, and life depended on one grand effort, expert swimming, which I did successfully, and after swimming six or seven miles, according to statements given by citizens living on the banks of the river, landed on the Arkansas shore without any assistance whatever. There I found a confederate soldier who came to my relief, and took me to a house nearby, and gave me something to eat, and I felt something like myself again, thanks to the Great Ruler of the Universe. The said confederate soldier worked hard to save the lives of the drowning men, and brought to shore in his little dugout about fifteen of them."

For many of the men, the only thing worse than being in the water was being out of it. That was true for Berry, who was at first happy to see a muddy shore to pull himself onto. However, what initially seemed to provide hope quickly became his torment: "Quickly shoving my plank into the water and starting for the place where the shore ought to be, which was the most foolish move of all, for when I arrived there and had palled myself up a small cottonwood tree I was surrounded by a perfect swarm of buffalo gnats, which made lively work for me, and although I had firmly seated myself upon a limb of the tree and employed both hands with bushes whipping them off my neck and breast — the only parts that were exposed — which were a solid blotch in less than an hour. Had I remained on a snag in the river I would have been free from the gnats and nearer passing steamers, by which I hoped to be carried away. I remained in this tree but a short time, perhaps an hour or more, when the steamer 'Pocahontas' came along, picking up all the men they could find."

As Berry's account indicated, the steamer Pocahontas rescued many men during the hours following the explosion, including Aldrich. He wrote of his rescue, "We had floated down the river six miles and lodged in the flood-wood against an island which was within two miles of Memphis, and here we were picked up by the United States picket boat, 'Pocahontas.' They poured whiskey down me, rolled and rubbed me, and finally brought me back to life. I was like the new born babe, not a raveling of clothing upon me, in a place surrounded by persons whom I had never seen before, but I was happy as a lark to think I was rescued and saved. They placed me on the stretchers and carried me to the Overton hospital at Memphis, gave me a shirt and drawers and placed me in a good bunk. The third day, as soon as I was able to get up, they issued a suit of Uncle Sam's blues for me and I was happy..."

Since their quarters were so near the boilers, few of the crew survived the explosion, but chief engineer Wintringer was among those lucky few. He also wrote of his rescue, "In a very short time after that who were picked up by one of the relief boats that came from Memphis and were taken to the city. There was supposed to be about 2,200 people, all told, on the 'Sultana' at the time, of which about one-half were lost."

It is unclear from the men's reports exactly how many ships were involved in their rescue. Berry remembered that he "soon attracted attention and was taken on board the steamer," which may or may not have been the *Pocahontas*, "and soon after landed at Memphis." Of course, as one continues to read his narrative, it becomes clear why he may have been a bit vague on the details of what happened, as well as just how poor communication was, especially in war time. He continued, "[I] was then taken to Washington Hospital (probably in Memphis, Tennessee), where my wound was poorly dressed, as I remember it, none of the broken pieces of skull being taken out. I remained here a little over a week, and although I gave my name, company and regiment to a reporter, and also to the hospital steward, yet about two or three months afterward my mother received official notice from Washington that her son was killed upon the 'Sultana;' and my name stands today upon the Michigan Adjutant General's Report for 1865 as killed by the explosion of the steamer 'Sultana.' ... After my brief sojourn in Memphis, I, with others, was placed on the steamer 'Belle Memphis' and taken to Cairo, remaining there over night, thence via Matoon, where we were obliged to wait a few hours for cars."

A drawing of the SS *Tyler*, one of the ships that helped the rescue efforts

William Boor also was taken to Memphis for care. He recalled, "When we arrived there the ladies of the Christian Commission supplied us with underclothing. I took an ambulance for Overton Hospital, where I changed clothes and went to bed and soon lost myself in sleep. Those of us that were able to go north were sent out of the hospital to the Soldier's home for dinner. In the evening about two hundred or more took a boat for Cairo, Illinois, where we landed on the following evening."

Few individuals ever go through something like what the survivors experienced that night without it making a lasting impact on their lives. Chester Berry, who later became a minister, recounted how his night in the dark water shaped his faith and his future: "Being now quite despondent, I had about concluded that there was no use of my trying to save myself, that I would drown in spite of my efforts ; and that to throw my board away and sink at once would be only to shorten my misery. I was just in the act of doing so when it seemed to me that I was transported for the moment to 'the old house at home,' ... I knew that ... if one of the family were away from home during the hour for prayer ... that one was especially remembered in the prayer. ... as plainly as I ever heard my mother's voice I heard it that evening ... when all the mother-soul seemed to go up in earnest petition — 'God save my boy.' For ten long weary months she had received no tidings from her soldier boy, now she had just learned that he was on his way home and her thoughts were almost constantly upon him; and for him her earnest prayer was made. I fiercely clutched the board and hissed between my now firmly set teeth 'Mother, by the help of God, your prayer shall be answered.' I started out for a grand effort."

Even before they had reached the safety of shore, some men began speculating on what caused the explosion. Obviously, after four years of warfare with their own countrymen, many minds were fixed on sabotage. According to William Bracken, who was among those rescuing the soldiers from the water, "On board the 'Pocahontas' were a number of soldiers belonging to the 113th Regiment Illinois Volunteers (the regiment to which I had formerly belonged), and they said that the general impression among the survivors was that the boilers had been tampered with, and that the boat was blown up purposely to cause the destruction of the soldiers on board. One or more of the employees of the boat were also of this opinion and they so expressed themselves."

In spite of these men's speculations, and those of others, there was never any evidence of tampering found. Had there been a more thorough investigation, something might have been uncovered. However, the war was over, the men were dead, and there was just too much else on the nation's mind at the time to devote the mental and physical resources necessary to solve the mystery. Indeed, they were never even able to determine who died on the vessel or how many perished, with an estimated 1800 dying, about 2/3rds of the passengers. Many a grieving family would know only that they had a son who had been in a prison camp and died, either in the camp or on the *Sultana*.

Either way, too many of them never made it home.

THE LOSS OF
THE *SULTANA*

Early on April 27, 1865, the overcrowded steamboat *Sultana* exploded on the Mississippi River near Marion, Arkansas. The vast majority of the *Sultana's* passengers, believed to number over 2000, were Federal soldiers, recently released from Confederate prisons. Approximately 1500 people perished; this remains the worst tragedy in American nautical history.

MARKER PLACED BY THE
ARKANSAS STATE SOCIETY
DAUGHTERS OF THE AMERICAN REVOLUTION
APRIL 1, 2000

Historical marker commemorating the Sultana in Marion, Arkansas

Memorial for the Sultana at the Mount Olive Baptist Church in Knoxville, Tennessee

Bibliography

Berry, Chester D. (2005) [1892]. *Loss of the Sultana and Reminiscences of Survivors.* University of Tennessee Press.

Bryant, William O. (1990). *Cahaba Prison and the "Sultana" Disaster.* University of Alabama Press.

Huffman, Alan (2009). *Sultana: Surviving the Civil War, Prison, and the Worst Maritime Disaster in American History.* Collins.

Potter, Jerry O. (1992). *The Sultana Tragedy: America's Greatest Maritime Disaster.* Pelican Publishing.

Salecker, Gene Eric (1996). *Disaster on the Mississippi: the Sultana Explosion, April 27, 1865.* Naval Institute Press.

The PS *General Slocum*

Chapter 1: As Fine a Day for a Picnic as Ever Was

Promotional material for the *General Slocum*

"There were several hundred excursionists already on the pier when the Slocum arrived. There were mothers full of pride in their lusty German-American babies, and full of anxiety for fear some of them would fall overboard in their haste to get on board the Slocum before anybody else did. A band came and went to the after deck and began booming out melodies dear to the German and the East Side heart. The mothers and children kept pouring across the gang plank and scurrying for "good places" about the decks. The Rev. G. C. F. Haas, and his assistant, the Rev. J. S. Schultz, stood on opposite sides of the gang plank and welcomed the mothers and the scholars. Policeman [Charles] Kelk and [Abel] Van Tassel, full of experience in the handling of Sunday School excursions, took posts on the off-shore side of the steamer, ready to dive after any towhead who by mischance should fall overboard. It was as fine a day for a picnic as ever was. The sunlight made the blue water seem as bright as though it lay anywhere but between the piers of the biggest city of this nation. ... Pastor Haas was good-natured, and it was well along toward 10 o'clock when the Slocum started, the band on the upper deck playing 'Ein Feste Burg 1st Unser Gott.'" – J.S. Ogilvie, *History of the General Slocum disaster by which nearly 1200 lives were lost by the burning of the steamer General Slocum in Hell gate, New York harbor,*

June 15, 1904 (1904)

It should have been a perfect day, the kind that the German immigrant families would look back on in years to come with delight and nostalgia. June 15, 1904 was a warm, mild day in New York City. Spring had begun to give way to summer and the trees and flowers around the harbor were in full bloom. Families from St. Mark's Evangelical Lutheran Church arrived at the pier early that morning, the women in their best dresses and shading their faces with parasols while the few men that had been able to miss work that day talked politics, well assured that New York's own Theodore Roosevelt would win reelection in the fall. Little children ran from each other and played tag while their older siblings tried to talk without being interrupted. There were over 1,400 people there that day, all from one of New York City's largest churches, and most of its members had turned out for their 17th annual excursion on the mighty passenger steamship PS *General Slocum*. As the Reverend George Hass raised his arms for attention and led his congregation in a rousing version of "Ein Feste Burg ist Unser Gott" (A Mighty Fortress is Our God), he had no way of knowing that within just a few hours, almost everyone on board that day would be dead, victims of the second deadliest maritime disaster in American history and the worst tragedy in New York City's history until the attacks on September 11, 2001.

Pictures of St. Mark's Evangelical Lutheran Church (now Community Synagogue Max D. Raiskin Center)

As the ship pulled away from the dock at 9:40 and the band played rousing tunes, Hass assured people on board, "I have worked hard to make this better than any excursion we have had before." They were heading for Locust Grove on Long Island for the church's popular annual picnic, and hampers of food were piled on the deck, as aromas of sausage and sauerkraut filled the air. Haas felt particularly blessed to have secured the *General Slocum* since it was considered one of the best ships plying the Manhattan at that time. The ship's captain, George Van Schaick, was famous for having survived the loss of the *Portland* when it broke in two during an 1898 blizzard, and he was also looking forward to an easy, pleasant day undisturbed by any significant problems.

General Slocum token in the collection at The Mariners Museum

Van Schaick

The *General Slocum* was still a relatively new ship, having been built by the Knickerbocker Steamer Company in 1891, but she was old enough to have been well run in and had more than a decade's worth of experience plying the waters around New York. According to a report written shortly after the accident, "The *General Slocum* was one of the best known vessels about New York Harbor. Since the time of her launching, in 1891, she has been employed in so many different capacities, and on so many different runs, that possibly five out of every ten people in New York City have, at some time, been aboard of her, or have seen her at close range. Built for the Rockaway service as sister ship to the Grand Republic, she was kept on that run during most of the days of the summer months, and during the thirteen years she has been in the service she has carried to that resort almost enough people to equal the population of this city. As an excursion boat she was easily one of the most popular of all the vessels that ply the surrounding waters. Her build did not permit of much room for dancing, but the younger folks usually found room in a rather small space on the main deck for this amusement, while the general arrangement of the vessel, with corners and spaces to suit every kind and class, gave her great popularity. During the excursion season, which comes before and after the Rockaway season, she was employed almost every day by excursion parties."

The report went on to praise the ship, which was said to have been a "boat builder's dream," adding, "[S]he was said to be unsinkable. ... She was a sidewheel boat, each wheel 31 feet in diameter, bearing 26 paddles. She had a steam, steering gear of the latest pattern, and was lighted by 250 electric lights. She had a speed of about 18 miles an hour. The General Slocum had three decks, the main deck provided aft with a comfortable and roomy cabin for women, and with a restaurant forward. The next above, the promenade, held the main cabin, richly lined with highly polished sycamore and upholstered in red velvet. Forward and aft of this cabin were roomy deck spaces. The band usually played on the after-part of this deck. The hurricane deck was provided with a running bench all along the outside. Her two funnels were almost amidships and were placed one on each side. Her body was painted white, and her funnels a medium yellow, while her name in large gold letters stood out on either side. She carried a crew of 22 men, a captain and two pilots."

However, there was a darker side to the *General Slocum*'s history, one that most of those on board that day did not know. The report noted, "The *General Slocum* has been in almost constant misfortune since a time shortly after her launching. No other vessel in the harbor has nearly as long a record of accidents as she, and she has cost her owners thousands of dollars at various times for repairs and for hauling her off some bar on which she had lodged. ... The officers of the Knickerbocker Steamboat Company have frequently been up before the authorities for over-crowding the Slocum. Almost every year special men were detailed to watch her, and charges against her were often made. In 1895 the company was fined $1,670 for a violation."

There were other problems as well, and they would tragically become all too apparent that afternoon. Although the ship had recently passed inspection, much of her equipment was in shocking disrepair, neglected by the Knickerbocker Steamboat Company and overlooked by the crew.

Nevertheless, as the ship pulled away from the dock, many standing on shore watched enviously, wishing they were also on board and heading for a day of games and good food.

Chapter 2: Real Danger

"Though Capt. Van Schaick did not know it, the steamer must even then have been on fire. Just back of the crew's quarters, up in the bow of the steamer under the main deck, is what is called the second cabin. On the *Slocum* this cabin has been used as a sort of storeroom. Spare hawsers and paint and oils were kept there. Gasoline was kept there, and it was there that Albert Payne, a negro steward, kept the ship's lamps when they were not in place, and cleaned and filled them.

Payne, his face ashy with the horrors he had been through, swore that he had finished cleaning all the lamps before the boat left her dock early that morning, and that he had not been in the room, except to see that everything was all right. He swore that just before the boat left East Third street the second cabin was all right. Along the Astoria shore, where there are many yards for the building of small boats, the trouble was known sooner than it was on the steamer itself. …it was quite a while after the Slocum was first found to be on fire that the seriousness of the situation was understood by all of her officers and crew. Very few of the passengers knew anything of the real danger they were in until the burning and drowning had begun." – J.S. Ogilvie, *History of the General Slocum disaster by which nearly 1200 lives were lost by the burning of the steamer General Slocum in Hell gate, New York harbor, June 15, 1904* (1904)

Disaster didn't take long to strike, because the *Slocum* had traveled less than half a mile when it became obvious that something was very wrong. William Alloway, the captain of a nearby dredge, notice a sudden burst of smoke coming from the lower deck of the ship, just in front of the smokestacks, so he sounded his whistle in an attempt to get the *Slocum*'s attention. Other boats also began to sound warnings, which alarmed people on board. Clara Stuer, one of the passengers, described the initial confusion: "I was sitting on the upper deck with Miss Millie Mannheimer, 40 years old; Miss Lillie Mannheimer, her niece, 9 years old, and Walter, the latter's brother, aged 11. We had just passed the entrance to the Harlem River, and were going slowly when Lillie called to her aunt, saying: 'I think the boat is on fire, auntie; see all the smoke.' 'Hush!' replied her aunt, 'you must not talk so. You may create a panic' Lillie would not be silenced, however, and it seemed but a few moments later when there was a roar as though a cannon had been shot off, and the entire bow of the boat was one sheet of flames. The people rushed pell-mell over one another, and in the rush I lost track of my friends."

Another child, a little boy, told the newly hired crewman John Coakley that he smelled smoke in a stairwell. Going to inspect the situation, Coakley snatched open the door to the ship's lamp room, a space full of oil and other flammable materials. Had he not opened the door, the hay that had been smoldering on the floor, perhaps lit by an errant cigarette or match, might never have turned into a full-fledged blaze, but the moment the oxygen came in, the burning hay turned into a potentially dangerous fire. To make matters worse, Coakley failed to close the door before rushing to get help, which allowed the fire to grow and spread at an alarming rate.

Although it took a few minutes to locate and identify the fire, the crew quickly jumped into action and might have prevented the disaster if the ship had the necessary materials with which to fight the blaze. Instead, the hose, which had not been used or maintained since the ship was launched, burst as soon as water was put through it. The men tried one more hose but found that it was similarly useless.

Van Schaick was informed about the fire approximately seven minutes after it was discovered, and at that point, he faced a critical decision. He could immediately turn the ship towards the shore, which was only a few hundred feet on either side, or he could attempt to reach a known docking place instead of running the ship aground. He later insisted that he feared the ship would be broken up on rocks if he stopped where he was, so he decided to proceed to North Brother Island, located about a mile and a half away.

A picture of North Brother Island in the East River

There was another issue, too, at least according to a contemporary account of the disaster. "It seemed to be the captain's purpose as he came up past 130th street to try to find a berth on The Bronx side of the stream. There are a number of coal and wood yards along there and some factories. Rivermen said that he might well have carried out his plan. The land forces of the Fire Department could have reached him there. But he said that a tug warned him off, telling him that he would only be setting fire to the shore buildings, and would not be helping his people in the least, if he ran in there. ...the *General Slocum*...turned again toward North Brother."

As a result, the captain pushed his engines to the limits and made for the island, but as the ship drove into the wind, it fanned the flames and made them spread faster. It also spread the fire directly towards those who were trapped on the back end of the ship. One account of the disaster explained, "It took Captain Van Schaick only a minute to see that he ought to get his passengers ashore as soon as he could. He determined on the North Shore of North Brother Island. It takes time to read of all these things. It took almost no time at all for them to happen. The yells and screams of the few people who were caught on the decks below the hurricane deck forward were ringing horribly across the water. The roar and crackle of the oil-fed flames shut these screams off from the frightened mass of Sunday School people aft."

WRECK OF THE GEN. SLOCUM, SHOWING BOX SURROUNDING THE PADDLE WHEEL. THE DOOR LEADING INTO THIS BOX WAS BROKEN OPEN AND MANY PERSONS WHO TRIED TO ESCAPE THROUGH IT WERE HURLED TO INSTANT DEATH.

Two policemen, Charles Kelk and Abel Van Tassel, were among the first to spring into action, and they were the only ones aboard with any real training in disasters or crowd control. Kelk subsequently provided a harrowing story: "As I was standing there, a woman came rushing toward me with her skirts in a blaze. There was a baby carriage standing near, in which there was a heavy blanket. I seized the blanket, threw it around the woman and rolled her on the deck until the flames were extinguished. She jumped overboard then, and whether she was saved or not, I do not know."

The two men quickly got the crowd moving toward the afterdecks, as far from the fire as possible, but passengers began to panic as the fire continued to spread. Mothers looking for their children became hysterical, even as Hass attempted to calm the crowd. 14 year old Herman Lembeck later recalled, "I was with my mother, two brothers and two sisters on the hurricane deck. We saw a lot of smoke and flames coming from below and mother got scared. Just then Dr. Haas, the minister, came running up to us. He said it was nothing but some coffee burning and begged us to be calm. He then went off looking for his own family."

After he had found what he believed was a safe place for his own wife and daughter, Reverend Hass spoke to his congregants, trying desperately to make himself heard over the growing bedlam, but sadly, his family would not be safe for long. In the aftermath of the disaster, he explained how he was separated from his family: "When the fire shot up to the top deck and drove the crowd back the panic was terrible. The crush from the forward part of the boat swept those in the rear along. The women and children clung to the railing and stanchions but could not keep their hold. I, with my wife and daughter, were swept along with the rest. In the great crush many women fainted and fell to the deck, to be trampled upon. Little children were knocked down. Mothers with their little boys and girls in their arms would give wild screams and then leap into the water. We could see boats pulling out from the shore by this time, and a faint ray of hope came to us. With my wife and daughter I had been swept over to the rail. I got my wife and daughter out on the rail, and then we went overboard. I was so excited that I don't remember whether we pushed over or jumped. When I struck the water I sank, and when I rose there were scores about me fighting to keep afloat. One by one I saw them sink around me. But I was powerless to do anything. I was holding my wife and daughter up in the water as best I could, almost under the side of the boat, when someone, jumping from the rail directly above me, landed on top of us. My hold was broken and we all went under together. When I came up my wife and child were gone. With a great effort I managed to keep afloat, but my strength was about gone when a man on one of the tugs picked me up."

Chapter 3: The Women and the Children Had No Chance

"There were scenes of horror on the General Slocum and on shore such as it would not be decent to set down on paper, even though any chronicler had the ability. It was a boatload of women and little children. For the last mile, when the steamer, spouting flames high into the air, was shooting swiftly out to the Sound with the tide, people on the shore and on other steamers could see the women and children fluttering over the sides into the water in scores. The river is swift there at flood tide. The waves grab forward at one another with hungry white fingers. A strong man would have but little chance. The women and the children had no chance. There have been heard such stories as often come out after a disaster — stories of cruel selfishness by members of the crew, of cold disregard of the Slocum's distress signals and most evident need by pleasure and business craft in the harbor. In the end came the story that there had been looting of the bodies of the dead. Some of these things were more or less true. But there was a glorious record of self-sacrifice and bravery to be set over against all that was evil or unmanly." – J.S. Ogilvie, *History of the General Slocum disaster by which nearly 1200 lives were lost by the burning of the steamer General Slocum in Hell gate, New York harbor, June 15, 1904* (1904)

J.S. Ogilvie, who wrote a contemporary account in the wake of the disaster, described the horrific scene that continued to unfold as the captain kept the ship moving upriver: "There was a puff like a great cough down in the Slocum's inwards. A red starry cloud of sparks and smoke and flames shot up and the greater part of the superstructure aft plunged forward into the flames.

How many hundreds of lives were snuffed out in that one instant nobody will ever know. Outsiders could see writhing, crawling figures in the burning wreckage, slipping down further and further into the flames until they were gone. …there was a thick clustering of women, all screaming, and boys and girls around the edges of so much of the superstructure as was still standing. At the very back Kelk, the policeman, was standing, catching up some of the smallest children and hurling them out at the decks of the nearest following steamers. Mothers threw their children overboard and leaped after them. When the stanchions burned out and the superstructure fell families were separated. … Now the big steamer, ablaze for more than two-thirds of her 250 feet of length, was rounding the point of North Brother Island. The flames were reaching out for the pilot-house. The door toward the fire was blackened here and there and the paint blisters were bursting with little puffs of fire. But the hundred nurses gathered eagerly on shore waiting a chance to help, saw old man Van Schaick and his pilots at their wheel, straining forward as though by their own physical force they could make the boat go faster."

George Kircher was one of the few on board that day who could swim, so he was able to make it to shore, but he narrowly avoided being crushed to death by the collapsing deck: "We had seats along the rail on the top deck, and we stayed together for a long time, hoping that some boat would come and take us off. The flames started in the front of the boat, and that made the crowd come toward us. It was awful to see them. I saw little children trampled on. Everybody was making for the back of the boat, and behind them seemed to be a big wave of flame. As the crowd from the front got to where we were the railing burst into flame, and then I had to jump. Just as I jumped part of the deck gave way and I saw the people tumbling down into the water through a big hole in the deck."

Meanwhile, as people began to grab the life preservers they knew they would soon need, another drastic problem came to light. One report noted, "On many of the bodies which were recovered were life preservers which seemed to have been perfectly worthless. Assistant District Attorney Garvan's attention was called to a collection of the Slocum's life preservers which had been made by Capt. Jack Wade. These life preservers were covered with such flimsy, rotten stuff that they could be ripped open by a scratch with one's thumbnail. They were filled with ground-up cork instead of with solid chunks which would retain their buoyancy. … There the scene was one of terrible confusion. Shrieking women, with little children clustering about them, were trying to get life preservers and fasten them upon their little ones. The men on the boat did their best to help with the life preservers. These, however, proved in a majority of instances to be death traps. Most of the life preservers were so old that their canvas covering was rotten and their fastenings worthless. Jacob Miller, an officer of the Sunday School, tried seven different life preservers before he found one whose fastening did not crumble and break when he put it about a mother of several small children. Other passengers had the same experience."

In the same vein, following the disaster, the *Brooklyn Eagle* observed, "It was confidence that sent hundreds to their death yesterday — confidence that the *General Slocum* was in trim, well manned, equipped with all the fitments for safety of life and rescue. The merest suspicion of such an awful tragedy as occurred a few yards from our shore would have led to a complete overhauling of the boat, to a test of her steering gear, which is alleged by some to have been at fault; of her fire hose and grenades; to an inspection of her galleys, or lamp room, where the fire is supposed to have started, and certainly to a substitution of real life preservers for the flimsy shams that were removed from the bodies. These life preservers are made of rotten canvas, that can be broken by the finger nail, and filled with powdered cork instead of lumps and sheets of the bark that would have had some floating value. The cords by which they are adjusted are as rotten as the canvas, and came apart in the effort to tie them. Then there were the boats. Little seems to have been accomplished by them. The crowds pressed about them so that only two could be put off, it is said. Yet every craft is supposed to be provided with enough of life rafts and life boats to carry off the complement of passengers and crew in an emergency."

Perhaps because the fire spread so fast, or perhaps because of outright negligence, little to no use was made by the passengers and the crew of the Slocum's lifeboats. Nicholas Belzer explained, "I lost track of my wife some time before the fire broke out, and was sitting on the upper deck when I discovered the ship was on fire. I drew my penknife and tried to cut away one of the lifeboats. I succeeded in severing the ropes, but when I got that far I discovered they were held with wire and were immovable. Seeing I could do nothing, I climbed over the edge and down to the lowest deck. I jumped into the river and swam ashore. The water was filled with floating bodies of those who had been drowned, and I had a hard time from being drowned myself by persons who would cling to me."

Making matters worse, many were caught completely off guard by the blaze and had no time to even try to find a life preserver or a lifeboat. John Eli, a 14 year old teenager on board, said, "My mother and my little brother Paul and I were with a big party from our neighborhood. … When we left the pier the deck was packed so with people you could hardly move. The band was playing, and we were all having a fine time. I was standing with some of the boys…when all of a sudden a big sheet of flame burst up through the furnace-room, right in our faces. My mother's dress and Paul's dress caught fire, and I grabbed them and started to run for the side of the boat. There was an awful panic; I was knocked down in the rush. When I got on my feet I couldn't see my mother and brother anywhere. The whole deck was on fire. I was swept into a corner and held there by the crowd. It seemed to me the people were going over the sides like a waterfall. The captain kept blowing his whistle, and I could see lots of boats coming toward us. I found myself in the water when the Slocum got near the shore, and I was picked up by a man in a gasoline launch. I saw lots of burned bodies floating behind the Slocum. Fishman and Gray jumped overboard and swam ashore. I haven't seen anyone else that was with us."

A picture of bodies that had washed ashore

In fact, the fire occurred so fast that the musicians barely had time to realize what was happening. August Schneider, the coronet player with the ship's band, was working that day and had brought his family aboard for a special outing. He remembered, "We were playing on the upper deck. The band, of which George Maurer was leader, was composed of seven musicians. We were seated in the stern when a whole crowd of people suddenly rushed toward us, shouting and screaming. At least half of them jumped right overboard. It wasn't until a few seconds afterward that we saw the smoke and fire. The wind, luckily, was blowing the flames away from us. I got my family together and told them to stick close to me. I took my little Augusta, 3 years old, on my arm and was just considering the best place for safety when the deck broke and fell with the ruins. I still held my child, but my wife and the other two children were torn away from me, and I didn't see them again, and do not know where they are. I was taken on by rescuers on a tugboat."

Many of the women aboard the *General Slocum* drowned, unable to swim either because they didn't know how or because they were weighted down by heavy dresses and petticoats. One survivor, Mrs. John Hynes, managed to make it and tell her story, but she lost one of her three sons. "I was sitting on the main deck at the stern with my son Frank, these two boys and a friend. When the smoke poured up I tied a life preserver on myself and ran upstairs, the boys having preceded me, to the hurricane deck. There we became separated, and I did not see them again until we met on the shore. I stayed on the ship as long as I could; then I jumped into the water.

There another woman struck me on the shoulder when she jumped. I held her up by the waist until my strength failed, and then let her go. She went down, and when she again came to the surface I grasped her by the hair and swam as well as I could with one hand to the paddle-wheel, where I held her head above water until a colored man swam up and took her from me. I don't know who she was, but I recognized her as a member of the church. I don't know whether she was finally saved. When I was relieved of my burden I saw a rowboat approaching, and swam to it, and was taken ashore. I had been there but a few moments when Theodore swam to the shore near where I was, and a few moments later George was brought to shore on a tug. I do not know what became of Frank. About three weeks ago he broke his leg, and was hardly able to walk. He was taken out for the first time to-day. I fear the worst."

Picture of workers on shore carrying a victim

Chapter 4: Making After Her

"At any rate, the General Slocum, observed now by hundreds of horror-dazed people on both sides of the stream and on the islands, turned again toward North Brother. Steamers and tugs from far down stream were making after her. The Department of Correction boat Massasoit was on the far side of the Brother islands. Her captain lay in wait for the Slocum not knowing through what channel she would come. From downstream came the slim, white Franklin Edson, the Health Department boat. Thence, too, came the sturdy little Wade, with her tough-talking, daredevil, great-hearted little captain. Jack Wade. There came also the tugs Theo and Easy Time, tooting their whistles, headed for the burning steamer. On board the Slocum horror was being piled on horror too fast for anyone to keep track of them. The fire, leaping now high above the framework of the steamer's hog-hack and roaring with a smoky glare of red tongues up thirty feet over the tall brown smokestacks, had begun to scorch the edges of the compact mass of women and children who were crowding back out of its way at the rear end of the boat. The greater number of these people by far were on The Bronx side of the decks. They seemed to feel, poor creatures, that small as their chance for rescue was, when it came it would come from the thickly populated shore rather than from the bleak, rocky, bare spaces on the islands on the starboard side." – J.S. Ogilvie, *History of the General Slocum disaster by which nearly 1200 lives were lost by the burning of the steamer General Slocum in Hell gate, New York harbor, June 15, 1904* (1904)

As other ships and boats in the river saw the *Slocum* was in serious trouble, many tried to rush to her aid. Aware that most of the passengers could not swim, the boats surrounded the burning ship and kept reaching out for as many passengers as possible, but they had to deal with panicking passengers. Bernard Miller, one of the few male passengers aboard that day, recalled, "Myself, my wife and four sons, whose ages were three, six, nine and twelve, were sitting on the first deck when I saw smoke coming up through the deck in great clouds. The people lost their heads. I grabbed life preservers and put them on my wife and children, and helped them over the side of the boat into the water. Then I put one on and went after them, telling them to make for the shore. The youngest child was in my wife's arms. All started for Randall's Island. I started after them, but had not taken more than a half dozen strokes when I was surrounded by a half dozen women, who clung to me and dragged me under. I had all I could do to save myself from being drowned by their frantic efforts to hold on to me. A rowboat came up and took us all on board. When we got to shore I searched for my family, but they were not to be found."

One of the rescue boats on the scene was the *Franklin Edson*, whose captain, Henry Eick, later admitted, "It is difficult to tell what to do in such an emergency as that which confronted us in the Slocum disaster. I had just left the Edson, which had come in at the Board of Health pier, at 132d street, when I heard five whistles from my boat. I was down there in a moment, and as I was going across to the Slocum the engineer yelled up the tube that he had water in three lines of hose. We soon saw that water wasn't needed, but quick work to save lives. Everything in the way of life preservers we had went overboard, and then the heaving lines. Fifty feet was as near as I thought it safe to go, for although the windows of the pilot-house were down in their frames I could hear them crackling, and the paint was blistering on the woodwork. Samuel K. Mills, the engineer, and William Balmer, fireman, did fine work. It was hard work in many cases, for there were several large and heavy women, whose weight was increased by their water-soaked garments. We got all those who came our way. Some may think that we ought to have taken the rescued ashore right away for medical attention, but I considered it best to save as many as we could. I think that we got about twenty-five in all. As to how many lived I don't know yet; ten, I am certain of, anyway. Six died after we got them aboard, although we did what we could to revive them."

Albert Rappaport, who was part of the crew of the *Massasoit*, a Department of Corrections ship, described his rescue efforts: "The first one I got was a boy who clung to me after I got back on board, begging that I would not leave him. He said he did not know where to go, as his mother was drowned. I was clad only in underclothes, and in a struggle to save another boy about thirteen years of age my clothing fell about my feet, and it was with great difficulty that I was able to get within reach of a heaving line."

Nearby tugboats also steamed over in an effort to help. The *Wade*, captained by a man of the same name, as well as the *Theo* and the *Easy Time*, were soon close to the mortally wounded *Slocum* and lending aid, as were two young men in a rowboat. In fact, Thomas Miley and John Kain may have been among the first to notice the disaster and immediately headed forward to help. Miley explained, "Both Kain and I were rowing, with our backs toward the Slocum, when we heard a loud report as if an explosion had occurred. When I looked around a cloud of smoke was hovering above the forward part of the steamboat. It seemed only a few moments until flames leaped up, but it may have been longer, because my companion and I were awestricken by the scenes that followed the explosion. We could see women and children struggling with those in the rear, and in their terror they clung to those closest to them and dragged them into the water. While this was happening the Slocum was being run in toward North Brother Island. She had been only 100 feet or so distant from the island shore when we heard the report, but in making the short trip, a long trail of struggling persons was left in the water. Many of them, I think, had been crushed to death in the panic before they touched the water, and they sank at once from view. In a short time flames burst from other parts of the vessel, and the passengers' panic became more terrific. Over the sides they were swept from the decks in masses."

Freda Gardiner, who was just a child that day, vividly remembered how quickly things on the ship got out of hand, but she also relayed how she was rescued: "We were all laughing, because my aunt had said she was afraid on such a big boat. When the first cry of fire came Aunt Louise told me to hold onto her hand, but the crowd came rushing at us and swept her away from me. A big man picked me up in his arms and held me in front of him, but he couldn't keep his feet. I fell over the rail and when I came up I grabbed a big piece of timber. A man in the water tried to grab hold of me and when he missed me I saw him go down. The rowboat came up just as I was about to let go the log, I was so weak."

George Gray had a similar rescue story: "I was sitting on the rear of the upper deck with Otto Hans…and Albert Greenwall…. We were just passing out of Hell Gate when I smelled fire. I looked toward the front of the boat and saw a big cloud of smoke. Otto, Al and I jumped upon a seat and grabbed life preservers. They were rotten and all the cork came out of them. Women and kids were yelling around us something awful. Just then a big blaze of fire came right up through the center of the boat and the people began to jump overboard. Some of the women threw their babies overboard and then jumped after them. The first tug that reached us was the Director. It was a big boat, and came right up close as we were going toward the island. I jumped on the boat and a lot of people jumped on top of me. Half of them fell back into the water between the tug and the boat. In a minute there were so many on the tug the stern was way down in the water and the bow up in the air. They kept on jumping and slipping off the tug and going down. I got hold of the leg of a little girl who was sliding off, and pulled her back, and then I sat on her to keep her from being pushed overboard. I saw a man on the upper deck of the Slocum throw a baby way out into the river and then jump after her. The baby's hair was all afire. The man went right down. Another man jumped over and grabbed the baby and swam with her to the Director, and was pulled up on to the tug by the captain. The baby was alive, all right."

As these experiences suggest, the tugboats proved vital in saving many lives that day. Gray continued, "When the other tugs came up everybody that was left tried to jump on them, and they jumped on top of one another. Lots of them fell off and were drowned. I saw some girls in the river swimming toward the island. They were picked up by rowboats. I saw two little girls who could swim sink when a big wave made by a tug went over them. The women and kids were crying and yelling so we couldn't hear the men on the tugs, who were waving their arms at us for us not to jump. I saw ten men jump into the river long before the tugs came, and not one of them could swim. They all went down. I thought the Director would sink or turn over when she started for the shore, there was so many on her. When we got off we were taken in wagons to the elevated road."

A picture of people looking for bodies in the river

Nonetheless, in spite of everyone's best efforts, many more lives were lost than saved that day. Bernard Miller told this harrowing tale: "Myself, my wife and four sons, whose ages are 3, 6, 9 and 12 respectively, were sitting on the first deck, when I saw smoke coming up through the deck in great clouds. The people on the boat acted as though they had lost their minds. I grabbed life preservers and after putting them on my wife and children assisted them over the side of the boat into the water. Then I put one on and went after them, telling them to make for the shore. The youngest child was in my wife's arms, and she and the three elder ones started for Randall's Island. I started after them, but had not taken more than half a dozen strokes when I was surrounded by half a dozen women, who clung to me and dragged me under. I had all I could do to save myself from being drowned by their frantic efforts to hold on to me when a rowboat came up and took us all on board. I searched for my family in vain. They were not to be found. We did not go over the side, until we could stand the heat no longer, and I was so long on the boat that I was badly burned about the hands and neck."

Chapter 5: The Rescue Work

"A HOSPITAL for the treatment of contagious diseases would not ordinarily be the place to look for heroism of the spectacular type, but there was enough of it shown at North Brother to give the place a name in history. Everybody took a hand in the rescue work — doctors, nurses, ward helpers, engineers, health inspectors and laborers. Even the tuberculosis patients rendered splendid service when so many of the excursionists were struggling in the water after the burning steamer had been beached. None of the other patients was allowed to assist, but many of them who were on the road to recovery volunteered, and there was much excitement among them. It is estimated that the island people rescued 150 persons from drowning. Commissioner McAdoo, accompanied by his secretary reached the island in the middle of the afternoon on board the police boat Patrol. At that time the lawn at the side of the main hospital was literally covered with corpses, and the police and others were fishing them out at the rate of one a minute. Three dead children, all roped together with toy horse-lines, were brought to the surface at one time. The Commissioner shuddered and raised his hat. Next came a woman with a baby clasped in her arms. The Commissioner raised his hat again." – J.S. Ogilvie, *History of the General Slocum disaster by which nearly 1200 lives were lost by the burning of the steamer General Slocum in Hell gate, New York harbor, June 15, 1904* (1904)

A picture of the facilities on North Brother Island

In the midst of the ongoing chaos, the captain and the crew finally made it to the river's edge, but by that point, the fire had spread completely out of control and there was no hope of saving the vessel or most of its occupants. Moreover, the captain was not able to get as close to shore as he had hoped to, so many of those he had hoped would be able to walk to shore jumped into water still over their heads and drowned. Miley noted, "By this time the shore had been reached and the Slocum had been run in between two small piers. Almost before the end of the footbridge reached the shore the shrieking passengers rushed out on the plank and we saw several persons drop into the water as though pushed from the sides. In a short time those who were uninjured were ashore, but there were some who had been hurt by the struggle for life aboard the burning boat who could not reach the gangplank. Some of the less frightened men rushed back and carried these to safety, but there were many, a tugboat captain told us, who had been hemmed in by the flames on the lower deck. This captain had run his boat alongside and picked up ten bodies and saved two little boys. The tug belonged to the Daley Company. The tug Wade was the first to go to the rescue. My companion and I followed and succeeded in recovering two bodies. One was that of an aged woman, and the other body was that of a boy, about 10 years old. The boy's head was burned and his face was bruised, as though he had been injured before he was forced into the water. About a hundred feet from the Bronx shore was a private yacht, with several persons aboard, but they made no move to help the struggling people."

As the burning *Slocum* reached the edge of the island, the boats that were undertaking rescue efforts were joined by firemen coming from all over the city. When the first truck arrived at the water's edge, it was obvious that the men would be able to do little from the shore, so the *Zophar Mills*, New York City's only fireboat, was called in to assist. According to one report, "She came up the river, screaming, with a voice that outscreamed all the other whistles which were being blown in every factory and yard from which the blazing steamship could be seen."

A sketch of *Zophar Mills*

Seeing that the ship was now more in need of rescue personnel than firefighters, the captain of the *Zophar Mills* pulled into the 138th Street pier and took aboard as many men from the Alexander Avenue Station as he could. One account of the disaster described the scene there: "When the Mills got to the General Slocum, the sight, as described by the firemen, was one never to be forgotten. Fire headquarters was informed of the extent of the disaster, and the fireboat William L. Strong was started for the burning Slocum. The *Abram S. Hewitt*, the Brooklyn fireboat, was ordered to proceed to Seventieth street, where she was met by Deputy Fire Commissioner Thomas W. Churchill, Chief Croker and Secretary Volgenau, who boarded her and were hurried to the place of the disaster. When the Mills got four powerful streams on the Slocum the remnant of the passengers, a hundred or more, were making a last struggle against the flames. They were together on the forward part of the boat, moving back from the onward course of the flames. Men, women and children were huddled on the bow, while those nearest to the flames pushed toward those on the bow. Each instant a human being was pushed from the railing of the boat into the water by the backward sweep of the maddened crowd."

The *Abram S. Hewitt*

A picture of the *General Slocum* on fire and a fireboat trying to douse the flames

Even at this point, J.S. Ogilvie noted that people were still trying to escape the flames on board the *Slocum*: "The great hulk was still burning like a furnace on top of the water. Living men and women were still rolling out from her decks. Hundreds sought shelter from the heat under the paddle-boxes, which seemed slow to burn. In there, among the wet paddle-blades, the rescue boats were filled again and again. … As fast as dead and living were brought ashore the weaker of the convalescent patients took them and carried them up on the lawn. There was a constantly increasing number of physicians coming over from the mainland, some of them in riverboats. Every burnt woman or child who showed any signs of life was carried into the buildings. The nurses' quarters and the doctors' quarters and the stables and every place that had a roof where cots could be erected was filled — except those in which there were contagious diseases. The dead were laid out in long rows on the grass. The living walked or were carried by them. Heartrending recognitions were there: women throwing themselves on the bodies of their children; children catching at their mothers' hands and begging them to "wake up," and screaming inconsolably when they realized that there would be no waking up."

Clearly, by this time the end was near, as there was little anyone else could do to save anyone. The report continued, "The crew of the Mills reported to Chief Croker on the tragic sight, when the General Slocum careened and went down. Men and women who had been crowded together on the bow of the burning steamer were precipitated into the water, struggling to catch hold of one another, and children could be seen floating away from the burned boat. The Mills steamed as close to the Slocum as she could and picked up those who could be picked up. Boathooks were used, and ropes swung to those in the water by the eager firemen on the Mills. Fire fighters dived to rescue women and children, and not a few of the rescued were landed by the Mills at North Brother Island. Chief Croker and the officials on the Hewitt arrived after the work of the fire had been done. Strewn about the face of the water for thousands of yards in all directions were articles of apparel — hats, capes, boxes which had contained luncheon for the picnickers, larger wooden boxes, burning wood, and here and there a dead body."

Meanwhile, people began to arrive at the scene from up and down the shore. When the owner of a marble works near North Brother Island heard what was happening, he shut down his factory and ordered his workers to go down to the shore, commandeer any vessel they could find, and take it out to rescue people. A nearby hospital also sent down all its nurses, and even some tuberculosis patients. One witness noted, "Delicate-looking young women, in the dainty white uniforms which nurses wear, ran down to the water's brink and waded in up to their necks and formed human chains, along which struggling, half-drowned refugees were passed."

Among the nurses who came to help that day was Pauline Fuetz, an 18 year old who was not satisfied at only being part of a chain. According to the same witness's story, "When Dr. Stewart, the superintendent of the hospital, sounded the alarm, Miss Fuetz was among the first to reach the beach. ... Fifty feet away the surface of the water was dotted with the heads of struggling women and children. ... 'I am going out to them,' cried Miss Fuetz, hysterically, as she pulled off her shoes and skirts. Several nurses caught hold of the girl and tried to restrain her. 'Let me go,' she cried. 'I can swim; I must go to their rescue.' ... Five times she reached the shore with her human burdens. The sixth trip almost proved her last. As she passed close by a woman, who gave no sign of life, the latter's arms suddenly clasped around the girl's neck. Those on the shore saw a short struggle and then both disappeared. They arose again, but Miss Fuetz could not break the woman's hold. Finally she placed her hand under the woman's chin and pushed her off. Before the woman could recover her hold Miss Fuetz had passed around and caught her hair and started to push her toward shore. When they were within a few feet of solid footing the woman suddenly turned and grasped the girl again, both sinking. Soon the girl's body appeared on the surface. Her strength had been exhausted. She was dragged ashore more dead than alive and sent to the hospital." When Fuetz was interviewed later, she would only say, "What could I do? I saw the women and children struggling in the water, and what could I do but go to their rescue? I was after the children. I wanted to save the women, too, but my first resolve was to bring the children ashore. The woman who got me nearly took me down with her. If she hadn't been so excited I would have saved her. It wasn't much to do. I learned to swim at Tisbury Park."

Not all the nurses there that day were medical personnel. Louise Galling was on board the *Slocum* as a baby nurse caring for her employer's young children, and she survived on basic instinct: "I had no thought, of what might happen to me. I had never swum a stroke in my life, and I didn't know the slightest thing about how I should begin. I only knew one thing, and that was that I must save the babies. So I took one in each arm and jumped overboard and kicked out with my feet and held them up as best I could. I did not care whether I could swim or not. I only knew that if I didn't I would not save the children. I struggled on through the water and got to the shore. I didn't know how, and I guess I never will, but I saved the babies."

Unfortunately, there was little else the nurses could do but rescue those floundering in the water, because the vast majority of the victims on the Slocum died before ever reaching shore. Even at this later stage of the disaster, though, there were some cases where skilled treatment or luck prevailed. Clara Stuer described how she was rescued and the horrible scene she encountered afterward: "Hundreds of people jumped overboard. I jumped over the rail and dropped down to the lower deck, when I began to dispense with my clothing so that I would have a better chance in the water. Then I started to climb down the side of the boat when I heard a voice calling to me to hold on a minute. I turned and saw a man standing on the bow of a tug which was approaching. I held on, and was soon taken off with a number of other persons who had been rescued from the boat and from the water. The tug then put into the landing on Randall's Island and after putting the people ashore went out for another trip of rescue. As I left the pier I saw what looked to me [to be] 200 bodies, mostly of women and children, along the shore lying on the ground. Physicians were working over many of them. In the center of one group I saw the Rev. George Haas. Several doctors were doing their best to revive him, and as I stood there he opened his eyes and looked about. ... I then searched about for my friends, and after a time I found little Lillie. Beyond being bruised she was all right. How she escaped she does not seem to know. All this time the boat was burning, being surrounded by tugs which were trying to extinguish the flames. Lillie and I then made our way to a boat, which took us over to New York, and we came down to Miss Mannheimer's house... but she had not yet reached home."

On a day marked by dozens of heroic deeds, few compare with those of Charles Schwartz, an 18 year old who risked his life to save 22 victims knowing all the while that his own family members, both his mother and his grandmother, had already perished. "I saw my mother and grandmother. They were floating face downward. I got them both ashore and helped the doctors with them on the lawn. 'It's no use' said the doctors, 'We can't do any-thing for your people, my boy.' I felt as though my heart would break, and then I looked out upon the water and saw that there were yet men, women and children who might be saved. A man came along in a little boat, and I swam out to him and worked with him. I went overboard whenever I could and swam up to people and helped them into the boat. Many of them grabbed at me, but I was able to keep off enough to prevent being dragged down. I felt hands way down in the water holding at my feet. Hands caught me everywhere, and above me was the fire raging and roaring. ... If I had been a stronger fellow I might have done a great deal more, but I'm light. I weigh only 123 stripped...too light, don't you think? Hero? Oh, I'm nothing like that. I happened to have the knack of swimming a little better than some other persons and so I thought it was my duty to do the best I could. Besides, I'm not thinking much of that kind of thing with my mother and grandmother lying there in the room. I did all I could for them, but the smoke must have suffocated them before they were in the water."

As hard as it may be to believe, less than 30 minutes passed between the time the *Slocum* caught fire and the last living person was pulled from the water. It took Captain Van Schaick about 10 minutes to reach North Brother Island and another 10 minutes for those still on board to swim to shore or be rescued, or to burn to death or drown.

At first, it seemed like perhaps only a few hundred people had perished, but then the tide changed and the channel began to give up its dead. The dead frequently washed ashore in pairs and trios, with mothers still clinging to children and babies bobbing up to the surface like rubber dolls in a child's bath. Those working on shore were forced to care for the living and place them alongside the dead; there were simply too many bodies to quickly transport to the morgue.

Eventually, the morgue itself was filled up, so bodies were laid out on a pier, awaiting discovery and identification by grieving families. Coffin makers and carpenters were called in from all around the city because there were not enough coffins on hand to bury everyone. They brought their tools and wood to the island and quickly assembled the boxes there. One writer observed, "Throughout the city there is mourning, but the seat of grief is in that section of the lower East Side, centering about St. Mark's Lutheran Church, in East Sixth street. As quickly as the bodies were identified at the Morgue by families or friends they were removed to their homes, and in this section there was scarcely a house without its somber sign of mourning at the door. There were few persons in the streets, which presented the appearance they might have on a quiet Sunday. Life there seemed at a standstill. When the survivors left their houses it was to go to the Morgue or to the church itself, where a bureau of information has been established, to ask for tidings of the missing; for in many families more than one went to death on the General Slocum — in many instances four or five, in some as many as nine from a single household. In a block of sixteen houses, eight were counted with flags draped with crape at half-mast."

Pictures of bodies waiting to be identified

Pictures of victims displayed in their coffins

While the light remained, divers continued to go down and bring up bodies, but eventually, the setting sun delayed their work until the following day. In the meantime, outdoor lights were brought in from around the city and set up so that the doctors and nurses could continue to work until, finally, the last survivor could be moved inside for treatment. The dead remained outside, but they were not alone. Faithful workers toiled through the night to make them presentable for their families, carefully removing jewelry and valuables and placing them in numbers bags so that they could later be claimed.

By the time the sun rose the next morning and brought the summer heat with it, the bodies were ready for their trip to the grave, but even that was overwhelming. According to one report, "The first of the funerals of the dead of the Slocum disaster were held June 17, and the bereaved parish of St. Mark's from which by far the greater part of the victims were drawn, was in the deepest mourning from end to end. ... There was a short service in the church, and the interment was in the Lutheran Cemetery, Queens Borough. There was no large gathering at the church to attend this, the first of the funerals of the Slocum victims. Few seemed to realize that the time for burying had come before many had succeeded in finding their dead. Of all the persons gathered in the church — and there were nearly a hundred when the funeral took place — there were very few who were not seeking news at the bureau of information which was established, of their missing relatives or friends. The search for the missing was kept up all day long, and even while other funeral services were being held in the darkened church and the hearses were carrying the dead to the cemeteries grief-stricken men and women were begging for some word at the church door, and in the majority of instances, learning nothing, would make the journey to the Morgue and seek again among the dead, then back to the church again to see if something had not been heard there at last."

A picture of unidentified bodies being buried on June 18

THE EXCURSION STEAMER GENERAL SLOCUM, DESTROYED BY FIRE, AND BEACHED ON NORTH BROTHER ISLAND.

[Photograph by the New York Tribune]

Pictures of the wrecked *Slocum*

Chapter 6: How Did Such a Thing Happen?

"'How did such a thing happen?' That was the question which was reiterated up and down the length and breadth of the city. People read of the captain who found at 110th street that his boat, with its precious cargo, was on lire and yet did not drive it to the shore until he was beyond 138th street, a mile and a half from the place where the cry of "Fire!" first reached his ears. Captain William H. Van Schaick of the Slocum explained, as best he could, how such horrible disaster had come to a company under his care and direction. He is a man 61 years old, and has had long experience in commanding pleasure craft in the waters around New York. Captain Van Schaick said that though he heard the alarm of fire early, he made up his mind at once that there was no certain place where she could be beached in shallow water south of North Brother Island. The tide was running up to the Sound with terrific velocity, and he was sure that he would lose time trying to turn his boat into a proper beaching place south of North Brother Island. He stuck to his post, although the flames scorched his clothing, until the boat was hard and fast ashore. Pilot Van Wart stayed with him." – J.S. Ogilvie, History of the General Slocum disaster by which nearly 1200 lives were lost by the burning of the steamer General Slocum in Hell gate, New York harbor, June 15, 1904 (1904)

Naturally, it did not take long at all for people to begin to look for reasons behind the *Slocum* tragedy, and, more importantly for many, someone to blame for their pain. In fact, the metal on the burning hulk was still smoldering when the *New York Tribune* opined, "A number of lessons will be found by wide-awake steam-boatmen in this disaster when the facts are better known than they are to-day. The chief one will relate to the prevention of any such outbreak of fire as that which occurred on the General Slocum. Another will deal with improvements in construction. In the meantime the public will do well to recognize the probability that travel on excursion boats during the remainder of the season will be safer than it was before. If no new precautions are adopted, at least a greater vigilance will be exercised. Again, the majority of the patrons of these boats also have something to learn about the safeguards provided for them by law. One person in ten, perhaps, can swim, but it is doubtful if one in a hundred can put on a life preserver. To make use of the latter in a crowd, and when a panic develops, may not be possible, but these hindrances do not always exist when the need arises. Many lives might have been saved yesterday if, before going on board the General Slocum, all of her passengers had familiarized themselves with the arrangement of a life preserver and the art of donning one in the right manner."

The New York Tribune on June 16, 1904

Of course, knowing how to put on a life preserver does no good when they malfunction, and as word began to spread about the condition of the equipment on the ship, particularly the lifeboats and life preservers, the *New York World* complained, "That so many persons should die in broad daylight upon a crowded harbor arm without fault of unpreparedness or such emergencies is inconceivable. The crew did as much as its numbers and its obvious lack of drill would, permit. …The captain may be criticized for driving his boat a mile into the teeth of a strong wind; but his was at least a trained judgment, liable to error but doing its best at a critical moment. For the chief burden of fault we must go further. It was in the boat herself; in her rotten and useless 'life preservers;' in her scanty equipment for fighting fire; but above and beyond all else in her construction, which fitted her and others like her for a fire-trap and for nothing else. This is no new discovery. The World has already, has emphatically, has repeatedly shown the criminal absurdity of 'inspection' laws that permit the officials to examine boilers and count passengers' noses, but do not permit them to question the safety of the hull except as to seaworthiness. Perhaps, with the lesson of this frightful disaster before it. Congress may now frame the legislation that has been so long urged upon it."

The New York World on June 15, 1904

Frank Barnaby, who owned the *General Slocum*, read these articles with great concern, for if fault was found in his vessel, he could be held liable. He immediately contacted his attorneys and began to gather together documentation that made it at least appear that the life preservers were indeed in good shape and that the only problem was that people did not put them on properly.

This story began to fall apart, however, when divers began bringing the bodies to the surface. Many of them were wearing properly affixed life preservers, only to still sink to the bottom of the river just as quickly as those who had none.

Barnaby next tried to blame the inspection system, agreeing with the *World* that not enough was done to make owners aware of the deficiencies in their vessels. He painted himself as a man who wanted to do the right thing but was misinformed by Henry Lundberg, the inspector who had most recently approved the *Slocum*'s condition. The *Evening Post* supported this accusation, possibly with some encouragement from Barnaby: "The *General Slocum*, bearing the inspectors' certificate of full equipment, had no effective means of saving her own hull from fire or the life of a single passenger from drowning. …we have talked with those who drew ashore bodies actually weighted down by the life preservers that Inspector Lundberg declares in an interview were 'in good condition.' We know that these life belts, when thrown into the water, sank like stones; when ripped open displayed a mixture of soggy cork and glue, no more buoyant than so much dirt. Now, recall that the fire hose which did not work, the life-rafts which could not be released from their wire lashings, the life preservers which came to pieces when they could be reached, and dragged down the unfortunate swimmers who wore them, had all been inspected and declared not only serviceable, but of the first quality. These life-belts, which possibly had never been buoyant, bore an inspector's mark of buoyancy from the factory, and the certificate of successive inspectors that no deterioration had taken place. Inspector Lundberg, on May 5 last, certified under oath that the life preservers were 500 in excess of the legal requirement, and all in good condition. He said yesterday that he tested all "that appeared in any way old," and did not reject one."

The men in question did not have long to get their stories together, because on the Monday following the disaster, hearings were convened to determine what went wrong. Divers who had previously been searching for bodies were tasked with searching for evidence, and according to one report, "Five feet of the fire hose of the General Slocum was recovered from the wreck by Diver Tulloch, and turned over to Coroner O'Gorman to serve as evidence at the inquest. The hose was burned at both ends and on a fold in the middle, as though it had never been unreeled. The hose is a two and a half inch canvas tube without any rubber lining whatever."

The same report went on to quote one former Fire Marshal who examined the hose and said, "The rough weave of the canvas on the inside causes a considerable loss of force at the nozzle on account of the friction with the water. Roughly, in such hose as that the loss due to friction would be about forty pounds to a hundred feet of hose. The hose is porous also, and leaks somewhat. That is, it 'sweats,' causing a further loss of power, until the fiber of the hose swells and makes the coating thoroughly impervious to water. That would take about ten minutes."

The report added, "From the sunken vessel one of the starboard steel lifeboats was also brought up. The boat was still attached to the davits, to which it was lashed by steel wires instead of ropes. The boat was crumpled up in the middle, as if it had been paper, and great gaps had been sprung in its bow. But boatmen say it would have been serviceable if it had ever been got into the water."

As the investigation progressed, Captain Van Schaick became a convenient scapegoat for many. When first interviewed immediately after the incident, he told the coroner, Joseph Berry, "We left the foot of East Twenty-Third Street about 9.30 o'clock. It was reported to me that 982 tickets for adults had been taken in at the gangways. This does not include children who came aboard, or passengers who paid their fare at the gangways. I should say there were about 1,400 souls aboard when we started on the trip up the river. I took the boat slowly up the river, and we were bearing over toward the Sunken Meadows after passing through Hell Gate, when I heard shouts of 'fire.' I was in the pilot-house at the time. I sounded the alarm for fire drill. Fire apparatus was stationed on the boat and the crew had been schooled in its use. I saw smoke issuing from the companionways forward, and my first thought was that it was coming from the boiler-rooms. I swung the boat over toward North Brother Island, knowing it was the safest and quickest place to land. Response to the bell in the engine-room showed me that the engineer, B. F. Conklin, or some of his assistants, were still at their post. A few moments before the boat grounded in the channel off North Brother Island the flames were licking the pilot-house. Followed by my pilots, I ran over the deck and jumped- into the river. My hat and clothing were burning when I jumped. I reckon the time between the first alarm and when we grounded at about five minutes. I floundered in the water and do not know who pulled me out as I neared the shore. Someone dragged me up under a tree, and it was some time before I was revived, I made the quickest and best landing under the circumstances."

Later, however, the captain changed his story: "I was in the pilot-house opposite Sixty-Fourth Street and saluted the Grand republic, which passed me at that point. I then walked aft to my cabin and stood at the door for a few moments, then went in and sat down. While I was sitting down the mate sent up an alarm of fire. We were then midway between the Sunken Meadows and North Brother Island. I gave orders to go ahead, and in three minutes the boat was beached on the shore of North Brother Island. If I had turned back to the Sunken Meadows the time I would have lost would have cost the lives of all on board. If I had turned and run to the Bronx shore or any other shore the boat would have struck head on and would have bumped us again into deep water."

Within two weeks, the grand jury had indicted Van Schaick and 10 others and charged them with manslaughter. Both Lundberg and Barnaby were acquitted, though the former was tried three times. Van Schaick, however, was ultimately convicted and sentenced to 10 years of hard labor in Sing Sing. His wife, unwilling to have her husband take all the blame for the incident, devoted herself to writing letters to President Roosevelt and then President William Taft until the latter pardoned him.

As for the *Slocum* itself, its tragic story had one more interesting twist. Enough of the steamboat was salvaged so that it could be converted into a coal barge, and it subsequently sailed for seven more years before ultimately going down off the coast of Atlantic City.

The grim fates suffered by the ship and so many of its passengers may not have been fair, but then again, history rarely is.

Adele Martha Liebenow, the youngest survivor of the disaster. New York Historical Society

A cartoon in the *Chicago Daily News* comparing peacetime disasters, including the *General Slocum,* to war

Memorial to the General Slocum disaster, found in Tompkins Square Park, Manhattan, New York City.

"IN MEMORY OF THOSE WHO LOST THEIR LIVES IN THE DISASTER TO THE STEAMER GENERAL SLOCUM JUNE XV MCMIV THEY WERE EARTH'S PUREST CHILDREN, YOUNG AND OLD"

Bibliography

Braatz, Werner and Starr, Joseph. Fire on the River: The Story of the Burning of the General Slocum. Krokodiloplis Press, 2000. ISBN 0-9749363-0-8

Kornblum, William. *At Sea in the City: New York from the Water's Edge*

Nash, Jay. Darkest Hours. Chicago: Nelson-Hall, 1976. ISBN 0-88229-140-8

O'Donnell, Ed. Ship Ablaze: The Tragedy of the Steamboat General Slocum. Broadway, 2003. ISBN 0-7679-0905-4

The SS *Eastland*

Chapter 1: A Foggy Day

"The captain expected a foggy day and began to study his charts in his room aboard the Eastland. He wanted to acquaint himself with the course to Michigan City, Indiana, not a usual destination for the Eastland. Pedersen had just passed Erickson, who was hurrying to his breakfast in the mess room. They had a full day in front of them. The busy summer season was half over. It was a Saturday, and the Eastland sat at the dock near the Clark Street Bridge, not their usual one on the Chicago River. They were just about to board twenty-five hundred Western Electric workers who were on holiday. They would leave promptly at 7: 30 that morning, on a two-hour cruise to their picnic grounds, forty miles away in Michigan City. The Eastland needed to leave on time. After Michigan City, it had to get up to St. Joseph to pick up another load of passengers, then return to Chicago, then back to Michigan City to ferry the Western Electric picnickers back to Chicago. ... Erickson sipped his coffee, unaware that the Eastland would not make any of those ports. Within three hours, he would be thrown into an underground jail cell with his watch stopped at 7:33, the exact moment he nearly drowned." - Michael McCarthy, *Ashes Under Water: The SS Eastland and the Shipwreck That Shook America*

July 24, 1915 dawned overcast but warm, making it a good day for a company picnic. Walter Greenbaum, the manager of the Indiana Transportation Company, was no doubt pleased with the deal he had put together for Charles Malmros and Daniel Gee of the Central Committee of the Western Electric Company to transport its employees to and from the site of their company picnic that day. The previous March, he had written to them that "we shall be pleased to handle your party on an excursion from Chicago, Illinois, to Michigan City, Indiana, and return on July 24. 1915. The excursion to be known as the Western Electric Company Employees Hawthorne

Works. The roundtrip rate of fare to be one dollar per adult ticket and fifty cents per child's ticket. ... We will furnish you five thousand adult tickets and 200 children's tickets printed in your name; also 5.000 pluggers for advertising. We would likewise supply you with 200 of our regular window cards advertising your excursion. ... Tickets to be good on our regular steamers leaving here at 10 a. m., returning from Michigan City at 4:15 and 6:30 p. m. We, however, agree to establish a special schedule for you on Saturday, July 24. 1915. providing you guarantee payment for at least 2,500 tickets, at the rate of 57 cents per adult ticket to us." The "Hawthorne Works" referred to the Hawthorne Club, a social and educational organization within the company.

Ironically, the initial contract did not mention the *Eastland* by name, saying instead, "This schedule will provide for the steamer *Theodore Roosevelt* leaving Chicago at about 8 a.m. and the steamer *United States* or *Rochester* at about 10 a. m., returning, steamer *Roosevelt* will leave Michigan City at 11 a. m., and the steamer *United States* or *Rochester* at 4:15 p. m., steamer *Roosevelt* at about 6:30 p. m." This is because the *Eastland* did not belong to the Indiana Company but instead to the St. Joseph-Chicago Line.

There were also some caveats that proved to be quite worrying in retrospect, particularly the one that said, "The Indiana Transportation Company reserves the right to cancel this agreement at any time if any new rules or laws be enacted, compelling material alteration of the steamer, increased expense of operating ship or causing reduction in passenger capacity of steamer below that of past year. Also in the event of Senate bill number 136 becoming operative prior to November 4th, 1915, or, at a date which would materially reduce the passenger carrying permit for the steamers heretofore mentioned."

Western Electric employees were not the only sightseers who would come aboard the *Eastland* that day, as the contract allowed that the "Indiana Transportation Company reserves the right to book other small parties..." However, almost everyone on board that fateful day was somehow related to Western Electric, and unfortunately, the vast majority of those boarding the *Eastland* that day had no knowledge of her checkered past. As it turned out, Greenbaum did, and he later admitted, "I had heard of it having listed one time in leaving South Haven several years ago. In leaving South Haven, I heard that the engineer had failed to put the water ballast in. In going into South Haven, they only had 12 feet of water. The Eastland would go into South Haven with the removal of her water ballast, and as they leave South Haven and enter on the lake they would put in the ballast. I understood at that time that the engineer had failed to put the ballast in and that caused her to list, and also the load on the top deck would have a tendency to make her list. ... I had understood that after this affair that she went up to Port Huron and that a number of alterations had been made upon the suggestion of Mr. W. J. Wood, the marine architect. ... They removed a number of the staterooms so as to reduce the weight that was up in the air." That said, Greenbaum also noted, "The fact that the boat was being operated was evidence to me that she met the Government requirements. The Government would not allow it to go unless it was fit. ...

I believed it was a safe boat..."

Later, much would be made of the *Eastland*'s ballast (the amount of water weight taken in or expelled to keep the ship balanced), and when asked about this, Greenbaum replied, "I know in a general way how tanks — ballast tanks — are usually installed. Every boat that carries ballast, the captain and engineer should constantly be on guard, if they have a large load of passengers to carry. I don't know what the Eastland carries. The Roosevelt and the United States have what we call ballast or trim tanks. ... On account of the depth of the water and on account of the landing at the dock, for the dock is high and the boat is low. They would let the ballast out so as to bring the boat up to make it easier for the passengers to get up."

Adam Weckler, the Harbor Master on duty that day, had always had concerns about the *Eastland*, and he later told those investigating the accident about a conversation he had once had with her Captain, Harry Pedersen: "[A]ll he said to me was — that was something that I could never get into my mind, I have tried to find out ever since I have been appointed harbor master — why the Eastland does not carry water. On account of the way she trimmed, she is always lunging on the side, she is never ready until the moment she ships off, she always gives a lunge according to the side she is tied, but I know the boat so well, I never was much — I know she doesn't carry water, that is why I have been trying to find out why she did not carry water, the only satisfaction that I ever got was they did not need any water. That they do not need any water. That is all the satisfaction I could get, they didn't need water. On the stroke they can fill their compartments in four to six minutes, they can trim her in fifty to thirty seconds. ...I would like to know from my own knowledge why they didn't carry water, I would like to know why, I have asked everybody connected if they knew anything about the boat, 'Why they did not carry water?' ... the answers had been given to me such as they have been anxious to get out, 'they are dragging on the bottom,' some excuses of that kind, still there is always mixed, there is something wrong with the working parts of the water ballast tanks."

Chapter 2: Shoes and Boots Clomping on the Gangplank

A later picture of the site of the disaster

"Passengers were issued tickets good for any of the ships. Those eager to get to the picnic early headed straight for the Eastland. By 6: 30, five thousand people were massing near Water Street, just outside the Eastland's dock. ... Most of the women, in their twenties and thirties, crowded near the dock with long-sleeve embroidered linen dresses. Their hats brimmed with apples, sprays of lilac, shirrings of striped taffeta silk, poppies wound in wreathes, and black velvet bows. Some had brims tilted in grace, others in flirtation. Men, lugging baggage and picnic baskets, wore derbies and straw hats, suits and ties. Boys in blouse suits and rompers held their mothers' hands. The girls wore dresses and bonnets or bows. They would all be funneled through a narrow set of stone steps between the street and the Eastland. With two inspectors using handheld clickers to count the passengers, people began boarding across the Eastland's white gangplank, four feet wide, eight feet long. They embarked quickly, about fifty a minute, polished shoes and boots clomping on the gangplank, which slowly began to dip downward, eventually a full foot." - Michael McCarthy, *Ashes Under Water: The SS Eastland and the Shipwreck That Shook America*

Joseph Lynn, Assistant Harbor Master, arrived at work that morning anticipating a day like any other. He recalled, "Coming from the south, I went down the stairway, working my way through the crowd of passengers that was endeavoring to get aboard the Eastland, and I went as far aft as the gangway, and they were taking passengers in when I arrived, and I found that they had closed the gangway and they were informing such as were waiting to come aboard to go back and go over to the Roosevelt, at her dock. It was understood between our office and Mr. Greenbaum of the Indiana Transportation Company that we would endeavor to facilitate matters by giving them bridges at any time that the other boats were loaded and ready to go through the bridges that ran inside of a bridge hour. I had made all those arrangements the night previous, and her hour was set for about 7:45, and previous to this I had been in the office of the Indiana Transportation Company and conferred with Mr. Greenbaum in relation to the hours of departure of these different boats — about live or six arrangements. The Eastland was to leave the South Haven dock at about 7:45; the Roosevelt at her dock at 8:15, that is east of Clark Street on the south side of the river, and the Petoskey to go from Wells Street, immediately after the leaving of the Eastland, and leave there at about 8:45, which would make about a difference of half an hour in time between the steamboats. And the Racine was to leave the Roosevelt dock at 9:15, and the Rochester from the Roosevelt dock at about 10 o'clock."

However, not long after he arrived, Lynn began to notice that something was not quite right. "I followed along after these passengers that were refused admission on the boat, until they were all off that dock, up over the stairway, on the approach of the Clark Street bridge, and when I was at her mid-ship gangway I looked over the side, and it appeared to me she had considerable of a side list, more so than I had seen her have at any other time that I have been down to the dock at the Rush Street bridge. ... I walked along there to where her spring line was, and met Mr.

Weckler, the harbormaster, and I made the remark, 'Ad, she has got quite a list' — we called him Ad — 'Ad, she has got quite a list,' and he says, 'Yes; it is a shame to let that boat go out with that load on her.' And I looked down the bridge at the same time, about, and saw Captain Pedersen there, and I says, 'Good morning, captain,' and he answered me back, and Captain Weckler said, 'Are you taking in your water ballast,' and he nodded and said, 'Yes, I am trimming,' and he left the starboard side of the bridge of the boat and walked out of our sight…"

Despite the captain's assurances, Lynn continued to be concerned. He later testified, "I noticed that the spring line was particularly tight, and I tested it with my foot; and I walked to her waist line. It wasn't in line forward and I noticed that it had a considerable of a side list, and I went forward to the head line, and it didn't seem long, and came back again, and I think that I had walked over the after gangway this third time, and back to the spring line again, and she had gone over four inches to my idea, what I had seen her former mark, for the water had gone down again, and I would say then she was very close — she had very close to an eighteen-inch list, from observation. She was down; her bow was pretty near off the dock, and the stern was in close to the dock to take the passengers down there. I went forward again to where I could look across her stem, and I leaned against the building, and looked up at her so that I would be perfectly firm, and wouldn't be swaying, and I saw her going, and I hollered to Mr. Weckler that 'the boat is going over, get off; if she goes, we are going with her.' and at that Mr. Weckler appeared by the stairway, and I heard' him holler 'Ed !' and I looked up and saw him coming out of the gangway…"

Believing the old adage that the early bird gets the worm, or in this case the best seat on the boat, employees and others began arriving at the dock at around 6:00 that Saturday morning, hoping to be among the first to board one of the three ships set aside to take them on a two hour cruise across to Michigan City. The picnic had sold out and more than 7,000 men, women and children were expected that day. Greenbaum explained, "My original intention was to completely load the Eastland before I loaded the Roosevelt. The afternoon before I called up McCleary [the government inspector] and told them to be sure and have the Government counters down to the dock and check the people ; I asked him to have a couple of men at each boat. I went over to see Lieutenant McMahon of the Police Department and asked him to detail half a dozen officers. He had a couple of officers at each gangway. She started to rain a little after 7 o'clock, and there were quite a number had a preference for the Roosevelt; the officers were holding them."

Daniel Gee arrived at around 7:00 and watched as his fellow employees boarded the ships, and R.J. described the scene on the *Eastland*: "The crowd was very big; it was impossible to get a seat or a chair. I was on the upper deck on the roof. … I should judge about 800 or 900 people. I didn't pay much attention. I looked but there wasn't a seat there, and it started raining and I went down. There were seats around at different places. I don't know; I didn't pay much attention. When I started to go down. I had to wait probably four or five minutes; it is a narrow stairway and the people were going up. I walked down."

C.C. Kelly and his family nearly didn't go, but they would find themselves caught up in the tragedy. He remembered, "When I first got here, I didn't intend to go to the Hawthorne picnic at all. But everybody seemed to look forward to it so much, and there was so much excitement over it, that I finally changed my mind. It took some time to persuade my wife, for she is rather timid about going in boats; but Harry Thyer's wife laughed at the idea of there being any danger, and finally got her consent. We decided to go out early and come back early, so that the children wouldn't get home too late. So by quarter past seven Saturday morning we had our seats on the Eastland. There were eight in our party - Harry Thyer, Mrs. Thyer, their two children, a girl, 8, and a boy, 7; and Mrs. Kelly and myself, with our two youngsters, Jenny, 9, and Charlie, who is five. We all sat on the second deck, as far aft as we could get."

George Goyett and his sons, Lyle (20), Frank (18), and Charlie (16), were also anxious to begin their day of fun. Goyett recalled, "We got down to the dock rather early. I remember looking at a big clock on a warehouse across the river, as I came out on deck, and noticing that it was just ten minutes past seven. Even then, twenty minutes before sailing time, it was hard to get a good place. I didn't bother to go to the upper decks at all, as I had noticed when we got on that they seemed pretty full. Lyle, the oldest of the boys, stayed downstairs, outside on the dock side of the main deck, talking to some friends. Frank, Charlie, and myself went up to the second deck. Frank went outside, just above where Lyle was standing, on the dock side of the boat. Later, when the boat began to capsize, they simply held on to the rail and climbed out on the upturned side of the boat. Charlie and I went forward to the ladies' saloon, up in the bow. Charlie went downstairs again, and I went outside to try and find a seat. The dock side and front of the deck were, I knew, so crowded as to be out of the question, so I went around on the river side. It was almost full here. There were two solid line of occupied chairs, one against the rail and one against the side, down the whole length of the boat; the space between these was filled with people standing and walking around. Seeing that there was no use trying to sit outside, I went back into the saloon. Charlie, who had come upstairs again, was carrying around a little handbag, in which were our bathing suits, towels, and some odds and ends. I told him to take it down to the cloak room and check it, to get it out of the way. 'You boys look me up when we get to Michigan City,' I told him, 'and we'll all have dinner together.' He went below with the bag. I never saw him again."

Of course, at 7:10 a.m., neither Goyett nor anyone else on the *Eastland* had any idea that they would be doing anything other than enjoying a nice summer picnic. He continued, "There was a chair over by the stairway, on the river side, so I went over; it looked like a pretty good spot, so I sat down. Opposite me was Wolcott, foreman of department 4910, with his wife and a friend of hers. They were sitting with their backs to the glass partition that separated the deck and saloon. Just then Miss Kathleen MacIntyre came in, with her mother and little brother. I told Miss MacIntyre to hold my place by the stairs, and went out on the forward deck to get chairs for the rest of her party. When I came back, we all sat down together. There were several other people around that I knew, and we had quite a little group."

As it turned out, Gee wouldn't even be on hand to witness the disaster: "All I observed was just a small listing, then I went to the corner of Washington — corner of South Water Street and Clark, I did not pay very much attention to the boat. I did not know that until I heard the people screaming and the fire department coming; that is the first. I immediately went and looked for my family. ...I did not see any people from the Eastland because my family was on the Roosevelt and the people coming from off the Roosevelt. I was very anxious to find out where my people were; I stood there until I seen them; that is all I saw. ... I did not see anybody from the Eastland at all, I was there after the accident happened."

Chapter 3: A Dreadful Strain

"On the dance floor, on the promenade deck near the rear of the ship, the young men and women began to laugh and make a joke of the rolling ship. As it would tilt, they would slide on the waxy floor, giggling and shouting, 'All together— hey!' The lines at the stern, near where the passengers boarded, were released and the Eastland's rounded back end began to ease out into the river. It was then that MacDonald, in the tugboat, noticed a dreadful strain on the three forward lines still holding the Eastland by the nose to the dock. From his vantage point, so close to the Eastland's pointed bow, he could see something almost no one else could: The bowlines, the only things that seemed to be preventing the Eastland from rolling over, were stiff, in miserable tension. Just then, Harbormaster Weckler came running along the dock and shouted to the captain of the Kenosha tugboat: 'Don't pull on her at all, cap. Don't pull on her at all. I am not going to give that fellow the bridge until he straightens up.'" - Michael McCarthy, *Ashes Under Water: The SS Eastland and the Shipwreck That Shook America.*

Lawrence Kramer was an office boy who found the *Eastland* already crowded by the time he made his way aboard: "I started for the picnic with another kid, who works in department 2063. When we got on the boat we saw how crowded it was, up on the upper decks, so we only went up one flight of stairs, to the second deck. It was pretty crowded even there, but we finally got a couple of chairs over on the river side of the boat. The part of the deck where we sat had walls, so that we weren't out in the open at all. We were sitting near the head of the stairs, at one end of a sort of alley that ran clear across from one side to the other. On the right side of this alley was the wall of one of the inside cabins; on the other side were the stairs, and then came the wall of another cabin. We noticed that the boat seemed to be tipping over a good deal, but we didn't think much about it until it went clear over. I remember we couldn't keep our feet, and kept slipping back toward the side of the boat."

R. J. Moore, who was aboard that morning, also described the listing of the *Eastland* minutes before it capsized in his testimony: "When I started down the stairs to go onto the boat, there was a long line, five or six abreast, and as I was going along the side of the boat, I saw water coming out of there; I saw it by the ton [out of] six or seven holes in the side of the boat toward the dock. ... I remarked to a gentleman, they were taking out a lot of ballast; he said. 'It isn't ballast, it is exhaust steam.' I thought it was throwing out a lot of steam. It was about 7:10, and the first indication of the boat listing was about eight or nine minutes before it went down, when the refrigerator in the bar was thrown over with all the bottles and made a terrific crash. I was on the second floor and could see the bottles on the floor from that end, and the boat started to list north, and if they were given a signal at that time, I think most of the people could have gotten off the boat. From that time on, the boat kept listing."

In his book about the disaster, Michael McCarthy wrote about what the captain was seeing as things unfolded. "In the Eastland engine room, Erickson noticed that his inclinometer, a little metal arrow that swiveled as the ship tilted, was leaning toward the dockside. Unconcerned, he ordered his men to open up the valves on the river side, the port one, to correct the ship's slight starboard leaning. 'Boys, steady her up a little,' Erickson said. In about three minutes, the Eastland was straightened up, and the gangplank was level for the parade of passengers boarding. All was back to normal. It was nearly seven in the morning, and the passengers herding aboard continuously had reached sixteen hundred. ... The Eastland rolled. As his inclinometer began to tilt from center to the port side, Erickson started up the engines to warm them. It was a slight tilt, and he guessed that the passengers, whom he couldn't see down in his engine room, were congregating on the upper decks on the riverside. To correct for the tilting to port, he ordered his men to open the valves to the starboard side tanks. Perfectly routine."

Adam Weckler, the Harbor Master for Chicago, was in charge of seeing that the steamer safely left port, so he had a tugboat standing by to pull the *Eastland* out. However, he soon realized that something was amiss: "I arrived down at the Clark Street Bridge at 10 minutes after 7 in the morning, and the boat at that time was listed to port, just coming over, about a 5 to 6 degree list. I stood down on the dock and called to Captain Pedersen on the bridge, and I asked him to put in his water ballast and trim her up. He said he was trimming all the time. In the meantime he had given the 'stand-by' order and cast off the stern line. The dock man ran forward to see what line he wanted thrown off. I would not let him throw off the line. I told Captain Pedersen to trim her up. He held up his hand to state that he was trimming as fast as he could. He stepped out to the outside of the bridge. The boat kept turning, and he shouted to the people to get off the best way they could, and the boat, I should say around in 8 or 10 minutes' time, laid right on the side. Of course, the people — passengers — on board were scrambling to get ashore. Those on the hurricane deck jumped overboard. ... Yes; she kind of listed about 7 degrees and came back again, and there is one man threw his coat off and jumped off the boat. I think two or three people jumped off the port side before she went over. When this took place, those people on the hurricane deck commenced to yell. I ran up on the dock and saw men and people climbing upon one another, and mostly all those people were thrown out into the water."

When Weckler was subsequently asked about what he thought went wrong that morning, he responded, "My idea is, sir, that there is something wrong with the pipes or pumps, there is something wrong with the machinery or the handling of them because they could not get them open in time. I do not think they took in water on the starboard tanks at all. I have understood from the assistant harbor master she had a little list to starboard and they trimmed her all over with the port tank; now in that case they had thrown the water from the starboard into the port tank and could not get it back quick enough, that is my idea. ...if you are unloading in the lake into small boats your rails high, you can take water ballast throughout one side and the other also you can load up the gangways and into small boats, you can control in unloading, you can do it in half a minute's time."

As the potential disaster was unfolding, Weckler was desperately trying to help the captain correct the situation before it got any worse. He explained, "He had given no orders at all, because he did not have time to give orders, he was standing on the end of the bridge, talking to me, when I was telling him about the ballast, and he stepped to the outside railing, with his hand in motion and he told them to get back. When she gave a lunge to port he yelled out, 'Get off the boat the best way you can.' That was after the stern line was cast off, this man ran up to cast off the bow line and the breast line...the tug was not pulling on the line, because the line was hanging in the water and the line from the tug, the boat, the bow, to the bow, in my mind, there was just about enough room for the tug to stand between the stem of the Eastland and the bridge. The tug between the stem of the Eastland and the bridge showed the bow line was up from the deck of the tug— there was no chance to pull on the line. To make sure, I gave more line on the tug and the line was hanging."

While there were many warning signs (at least in retrospect), when the disaster occurred, it caught everyone by surprise. In his formal statement, Captain Harry Pedersen claimed, "I was on the bridge and was about ready to pull out when I noticed the boat begin to list. I shouted orders to open the inside doors nearest the dock and give the people a chance to get out. The boat continued to roll and shortly afterwards the hawsers broke and the steamer turned over on its side and was drifting toward the middle of the river. When she went over I jumped and held onto the upper side. It happened in two minutes. The cause is a mystery to me. I have sailed the lakes for twenty-five years and this is the first serious accident I ever had. I do not know how it happened."

Chapter 4: The Boat's Tuning Over

"Then MacDonald saw something that he hadn't seen in all his thirty-one years. Six men on the top deck of the Eastland dashed to the dockside railing. They had decided to make a break for it, and leapt overboard, grabbing a hold of one of the four-inch-thick Manila ropes lashed from the bow of the Eastland to the dock. Hands hooked on it, they began crossing the fat line, called a hawser, hand over hand, monkeylike, suspended above the river. Inside the tilting ship, the mandolin players and violinists struggled to play, and began to dig their heels into the floor to keep from slipping. The Eastland leaned farther. In the engine room, a chute the black gang used to discharge ashes suddenly dipped under water. The river began to gush in. Some of the stokers and oilers hightailed it up steel ladders and fled with sooty faces. On the tugboat, MacDonald was alarmed to see water starting to gush into the partly opened gangways, the square doorways used to load cargo and passengers. Before he could even shout a warning, one of the bowlines, pulling and pulling on a massive stake, lifted the timber piling right out of the dock. Then a second dock line snapped. 'Get off— the boat's turning over,' shouted Mike Javanco, who was rolling his vegetable wagon across the Clark Street Bridge." - Michael McCarthy, *Ashes Under Water: The SS Eastland and the Shipwreck That Shook America.*

Bob Satterfield's illustration depicting the *Eastland* capsizing

Just before 7:30 a.m., with more than 2,500 passengers crowding the ship, matters went from bad to worse when the *Eastland* finally began to actually capsize. Algernon Richey, who saw the accident from the safety of land, noted, "[The captain] stood on the right-hand side of the bridge, with his hand on the rail. As she went over, he grabbed it with his left hand and climbed over, and never even got his feet wet. At the time she started to list, when the captain gave his orders — after she listed at a 45 degree angle; the passengers on the hurricane deck rolled toward that side. ...the people that were on the river side — the port side of the boat — as she stood there, gradually listing to that side there, after it got to the top of the freight deck door — then there were cries and screams and she went down like that."

George Haber was fortunate enough to witness the accident from the safety of land. He explained, "I was standing on the dock less than 100 feet away when the boat began to turn over. Some on the men on the boat were loosening some of the ropes. I noticed one heavy cable still fast to the stern, though. Then the boat began turning. It was perhaps ten minutes in turning over on its side. There were about 150 persons I should judge, on the upper decks and from the number that had gone on board, there must have been many more than that below."

L. D. Gadroy, one of the ship's passengers, discussed the exact instant the ship began to capsize: "It was about 7:10 this morning and the boat was lying at the dock near Clark Street Bridge loading with passengers. We were to leave is twenty minutes and the upper deck and cabins were crowded with passengers. There were hundreds of women and children. I estimate there were between two and three thousand on the boat at the time of the accident. I was standing on the tower deck near the gang plank watching the people come aboard. Suddenly I noticed the boast list toward the center of the river. It rolled slightly at first and then seemed to stop. Then it started to roll again. I became alarmed and shouted to the crowd to keep still. Apparently a majority of the passengers were on the side of the boat and this had overweighed it and caused it to list. Suddenly the hawsers which held the boat to the dock snapped and the officers pulled the gang plank in and refused to allow any more on the boat. At this time everybody was panic stricken. Women screamed and men tried to quiet them. I attempted to reach an upper deck but could not because the crowd and the excitement and ran back to the port side, where the gangway had been. The boat then slowly drifted away from the dock, rolling as it slipped in the mid-stream and a moment later it had turned over on its side.

Mrs. Etta O'Donnell believed (probably erroneously) that the gangplank had been holding the ship in place all along. She told a reporter, "The steamer was getting ready to leave and was crowded with excursionists. The officers of the boat pushed the crowd back, which was around the gang plank in order to pull it in. I think this was what caused the boat to list to one side. It never stopped when it started to roll and a few moments later it was out in the middle of the river on its side. I saw dozens of people drowned around me, but was unable to give assistance. By a great effort I was able to climb on the upper side of the boat and managed to hold on until rescued."

Regardless of the cause, within seconds, cries of joy turned into screams of terror as it became clear that people's survival depended almost entirely on where they were at the time the steamer began to turn over. C.C. Kelly, who almost hadn't attended the picnic, described his group's predicament: "Luckily for us, as it afterwards turned out, we were back of the cabin, so we escaped being trapped. When the boat began to list, I didn't think much of it, for I knew that they often rock like that when they are starting up. And then, all of a sudden, she went over. We all went pretty far under the water, of course. I was the first to come up, and found that we were in a regular cage. The stern rail was on the right, the rear wall of the cabin of the left, and the floor and roof of the deck in front and back. There was a lot of loose stuff floating around, and when my wife came to the surface, she came right up under a heavy chair. She got out from under it somehow, and when I saw her I called, 'Where are the children?' 'I don't know,' she said. Just then my little girl came up near me. There was no sign of the boy, though, and I had almost given him up when I saw his hand coming up through the water right by me. Maybe I didn't grab it! All this couldn't have taken half a minute, but it certainly seemed longer."

As everyone on board realized they were in serious trouble, there was mass panic. R.J. Moore recalled, "I tried to get on the south side; there were a little batch of ladies and children, and I took a chance and went with the crowd. I went through the staircase, and just as I struck the floor, the water struck me. I got up in some part of the boat and worked my way through — I suppose about the width of this umbrella and maybe fourteen feet long; it was filled with women and children. They were all saved. I don't know if any of them are here or not. I was pulled out second to last by one of the firemen. I think he belonged to a tugboat. I hung on down in there for thirty-five minutes before I was taken out. When I came out. I wandered away; my clothes were all torn and I was dazed."

According to young Lawrence Kramer, "The soda fountain was near where we were, over beyond the stairs, and that broke loose and fell down on a lot of people that were piled up near me. When I came up out of the water I could see the portholes of the dock side of the boat right over my head. I got over to the wall of the cabin ahead of the stairs, and stood up on that. There were portholes in the side of that cabin too, and you could see the people who were caught inside. They'd come up to the surface of the water, and look at you, and then they'd go down again. Gee, it was awful! When the boat started to go over, the other kid got over to the other side and hung on to one corner of the cabin that was toward the back of the boat. But a man fell down on top of him and knocked him into the water. After he came up he got over to where I was standing out of the water, and climbed up with me. The ceiling of the deck was behind us, and it had cross beams on it. So we crawled up that. I'd boost him, and he'd pull me up to where he was. When we got up to the top, we could just stick our heads out of the porthole, by reaching over. The other kid went through, and then I got hold of the edge of the porthole and swung over. There was a bench under the porthole, and I got one foot on that, and that steadied me. I managed to get half way through the porthole, and then a fireman pulled me through the rest of the way."

A picture of the capsized *Eastland*, with rescue workers attempting to save people while onlookers watch from land

John Morey's life was spared primarily because of where he was at the time the ship tilted. "I was on the upper deck when the boat began to list. I though the boat was rocking at first, then it kept on turning on one side. I caught hold of the rail and held on as the boat went over on its side. A loose chair swung around and struck me on the forehead. Something else hit me, but I don't know what it was, but I managed to keep my feet on the rails until rescued. There were more than 500 on my side of the boat at the time, and many of them must have been drowned."

Obviously, the primary response of the passengers was one of shock and terror. Henry Vantak remembered, "I could not believe the boat was turning over. About a dozen of the 150 persons on the upper decks jumped. The rest were thrown into the river. I did not see my wife or children after the boat turned. They were carried into the river with the crowd. Someone grabbed me around the neck and kept pulling me. It was a woman, but I could not save her."

Few situations in human experience could be more terrifying than being trapped underwater, and tragically, that was the situation that many of passengers on the Eastland found themselves in. Goyett wrote about the chaos around him:

"I had just about sat down when the boat began to list. It went over so far that my chair slid away from the stair rail, against which I was leaning. I didn't pay much attention to this - simply pushed my chair back again. Then the Eastland began to go over in earnest. I caught hold of one of the stair posts and managed to keep from sliding. I looked over to where the people had been sitting on the dock side of the saloon and outer deck. What I saw was exactly what you see when you watch a lot of children rolling down the side of a hill. That entire crowd of men, women and children came slipping and sliding and sprawling down with a mass of lunch boxes, milk bottles, chairs - rubbish of all sort - on top of them. They came down in a floundering, screaming mass, and, as the boat turned completely over on its side, crashed into the stairs, carrying them away. The whole thing came down on me, of course, and I was carried down to the river side of the saloon, which by this time was full of water. I happened to fall against one of the posts between the glass partitions; otherwise I would have gone right down to the river bottom.

"Just as I slid down I managed to retain enough presence of mind of jam a handkerchief in my mouth, to keep from swallowing any water. I lay doubled up there, unable to move, for what seemed years, until the water had risen high enough to float the wreckage off me. I probably owe my life to the fact that a chair was jammed in above me which saved me from being crushed under the weight of the others who had fallen down. I don't remember being frightened - there wasn't time. I know that I was absolutely sure that I was going to be drowned. There didn't seem to be the slightest hope of my being able to get out alive. It sounds like a joke to say that I remembered everything wrong that I had ever done in my past life; that is supposed to be a myth that is always told about drowning people. But that is exactly what happened to me. At last the pressure began to ease up, and I was able to come up to the surface and keep afloat by treading water. The air pressure in the saloon was fearful, and it was some time before I could breathe properly. The boat was lying on its port or left side. Consequently, as I floated facing the dock, I had the glass partition forming the starboard wall of the saloon over my head, the ceiling in back of me, the port side and the river bottom under me, and the saloon deck in front of me."

Desperately searching for a way to survive, Goyett began assessing his situation. He continued, "I worked my way back until I bumped into the saloon ceiling. This consisted mainly of life preserver racks, so I managed to get my feet on one of the cleats, and, holding on to another, was able to keep my head out of water without treading. I looked around the saloon. Several people were floating around, alive. Among them were five of our girls. I called to them, and they managed to get over to where I was. By resting their hands on my shoulders they were all able to keep afloat without much exertion; they kept remarkably cool. In fact, the only person who had lost self-control was a poor woman to my left, who was also clinging to the life-preserver racks. Her child had fallen out of her arms when the boat went over, and was somewhere down under the wreckage. She was frantic, and kept screaming, 'Where's my baby!

Where's my baby!' Over toward the stairs I caught sight of Wolcott with his wife. I called out to him, 'Tom, are you hurt?' 'No, I'm all right,' he answered, 'she has a piece of railing to hang on to.'"

EASTLAND OVERTURNED IN CHICAGO RIVER 7/24/15   3555-7

A picture of the overturned *Eastland*

Chapter 5: Soaked Corpses

"A slate sky. The tugs tilted under the weight of soaked corpses being lifted quickly from the murky water. Among those at the river, some bystanders had had an impulse to jump into the chilly river and help, then thought the better of it. ... Another man, the one who was supposed to supervise the swimming races at the picnic and who was an expert swimmer himself, swam back and forth for more than half an hour rescuing others. Then, exhausted, he drowned. The sinking just an hour old, the Iroquois Memorial Hospital and other area hospitals were overwhelmed with injured survivors, and ambulances were racing from the bridge to outlying hospitals. For blocks, the streets were jammed, with thousands milling shoulder to shoulder, and cars threading through them. ... A stream of trucks and horse-drawn wagons made its way through the crowds, bringing lung motors, tubes, and respiratory equipment. The machines were switched on and rumbled and clanked in a ghostly symphony. A doctor from the Red Cross injected the retrieved bodies, some with eyes closed, some with eyes open, with strychnine, a stimulant. At one point, the drug seemed to spark some life in one man, and the respirators were used to try to pump the breath of life back into him." - Michael McCarthy, *Ashes Under Water: The SS Eastland and the Shipwreck That Shook America.*

From almost the moment the *Eastland* capsized, rescue efforts were underway both from land and on the water. Seeing what was happening, Richey tried to help from his vantage point on land. "I stood with the bridge tender of the railroad company at the north end of the Clark Street Bridge from 7 o'clock on until she went over. I saw her start to list. We commented upon it in every way, commented upon it until it got to the top of the middle deck doors. She got to the top of that and commenced to list more, fast, and the crowd on the boat deck, the hurricane deck, started to the south; they ran to the south rail, starboard side. They ran over and it seemed their feet — probably the boat went faster; she went down quick after that. It seemed as if she were overbalanced at the time. ... Those between decks were penned in underneath. ... I ran over to the middle of the bridge and called to the captain. ...he was on the bridge. I ran over and called to him that the boat was listing and that she was going over, after she got to the freight deck doors. ... The bridge tender and I ran down on the pier on the bridge. We threw in everything we could find that was loose; went down on the dock on the south side of the river; the ship chandlers there threw out coil after coil of rope ; we made them fast and threw them into the river, and pulled out three, four and five at a time. I am a good swimmer myself, even with one hand, but I didn't dare go into the water. They would take one — even a good swimmer; those who came up would grab him, three or four of them."

As soon as he understood what was happening, Lynn, the Assistant Harbor Master, sprang into action to try to summon help. "My first impulse was to get back to a telephone, which I did. And I ran up the stairs on the approach of the bridge, south to the iron bridge, and goes back to the City of South Haven dock, and, arriving on the first floor, I had to go west 150 feet, then back to get up another flight of stairs, and then came in here and got into the South Haven steamboat line's office, and I got a telephone and immediately telephoned the City Hall and had them send all the ambulances and pulmotors and lung motors, and to notify the police department and the fire department that the Eastland was turning over, and that is about an interval of nine or ten minutes from the time I landed on that dock, and I set the telephone down and looked out, and saw that the tug was in close under her bow, and that they were jumping onto that, and the people were climbing over her side — the starboard side — in over the side, and some were jumping out into the river, and throwing life preservers and other things, and the dock men were throwing everything..."

At this point, Lynn made a quick decision that might not have saved many lives but at least represented an attempt to do something that could have made a big difference. "I grabbed a telephone book, hunting for the city boat company, to come and cut holes in her — upon her — between what you would call her second, you would call that the second main deck — that is, her cabin deck. An opportunity to get out would have to be through those portholes — those on the starboard side were going over the rail to get on her side and stand on them, and I tried to look at it, and I didn't know where to look for it, for those ox-welders, because they had to cut places for them in order to get down into the cabin, and I tried the big phone — the regular day company's phone, thinking that they had one over there, and I asked where to get them, and I couldn't get that office, and I came back down onto the dock to assist in throwing all the lines that I possibly could, brought from the docks. The yardmaster — probably he was there, and every description of things over to the boat, and endeavoring to get those people quieted, and to throw the lines around the river side of this to those who were in the water, and went over to La Salle street, then to South Water, down South Water to Wells and across the Wells Street bridge down the dock to the Dunham Towing Company, to inquire if they had such a thing there, and I was unable to get this tug company on the phone."

With more than 2,000 people suddenly plunged into the cold water, pandemonium ensued, and policeman Henry II. Scalier was one of the first men to come to their rescue. "I saw scores of men and women, many of them holding children, plunge into the water. I jumped into a row boat and I pulled out to the drowning. I think I got about fifty ashore. The fire boat and tugs hurried to the scene and picked up more than a hundred people. We grabbed those nearest us first. At one time I had four women in the boat with me. Others I aided by dragging them from the water onto the decks."

Gadroy was one of the fortunate ones. He recalled, I climbed over on the side of the boat and stayed there until I was taken out by life savers. Many of the passengers leaded into the water as the boat went over. Scores of others were caught in the cabins and drowned. When the small boats began coming out to us, I worked with other survivors in taking passengers out of the water and cutting holes in the cabins to remove bodies."

Joe Brozak survived thanks to an incredibly lucky accident: "I was with a party of four and they were all drowned. My coat caught on a nail and when the boat went over I was held above the water." Meanwhile, C. C. Kelly and his family were eventually rescued: "We managed to hold on to an angle iron, and I shouted for help. Before long, they let down ropes and got us out. Mrs. Thyer and her boy were saved; but Harry and the little girl were lost. The girl was sitting holding my daughter by the hand as the boat went over, and I can't imagine how they were separated. When I got out and looked at my watch, I found it had stopped. I haven't wound it since. It's just as it was then, with the hands pointing to seven thirty-one."

Goyett lost his youngest son in the wreck, but he and his two older sons survived, and he told the story of his rescue. "Just then the first of the rescuers found us. Someone stuck an oar through the porthole over our heads nearby. The woman who had lost her baby made a grab for it, missed it, and went down. I managed to grab her and get her back beside me, and tried to quiet her. The only way the rescuers could get at us was by smashing the glass partition over our heads. Of course, all the jagged pieces of glass showered down of top of us, and several of us were cut - I had one of my thumbs gashed; but it was the only thing to do. They let a rope down with a loop on the end of it, and we threw it over the shoulders of the woman who had gone under before. She was the first one to be pulled out. When all the women were out I must have caved in all at once. I remember hearing someone call down, 'Come out yourself, George.' I remember, too, trying to put the rope under my shoulders. I must have succeeded, for the next thing I remember is lying out on the side of the boat with an ambulance surgeon down beside me. I tried to get up, but found that my right leg wouldn't hold me. 'How do you feel?' the surgeon asked me. 'Pretty good,' I said, 'but I can't walk.' The surgeon looked me over and said I had a dislocated knee. So a big policeman held on to my upper leg while the surgeon pulled on the lower and snapped the joint into place. It certainly felt fine after it got back! I felt perfectly well, and said I thought I'd go back and help get some of the other people out. 'Not much you won't,' said the surgeon. And before I knew it they had me in an ambulance, on the way to the Iroquois Hospital."

As the luckiest survivors were able to get clear of the ship and others were rescued by the nearby tugboat *Kenosha*, others continued to help on land. Among those on hand to try to help was a nurse named Repa, who later explained how she arrived on the scene: "I was on a trolley car, at Lake Street, when I heard what I thought must be screams; I could hear them even above the noise of the car and the noises on the street. Just then a mounted policeman galloped up and stopped all the traffic, shouting: 'Excursion boat upset - look out for the ambulance!' I knew at once that it must be one of our boats, and ran to the front of the car, to get off. The motorman tried to stop me, but I slipped past him and jumped off just as one of the ambulances came up. It had to slow up on account of the congestion, and I managed to jump on the back step. I had my uniform on, and so was allowed to stay on until we got to the dock. I don't know how I got on the dock, or on the Eastland. Indeed, there are a good many things that happened that day that I am still hazy about. All I remember is climbing up the slippery side of the boat, losing my footing, and being shoved up by somebody from behind. I finally got to where I could stand up on the side of the boat, which was lying out of water."

A picture of the Kenosha rescuing passengers

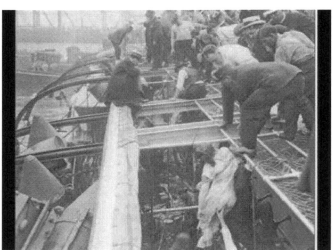

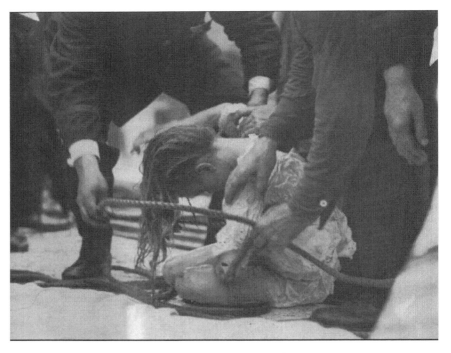

Pictures of the frantic rescue efforts

Even for someone with a strong medical background, the scene at the dock was shocking. Repa wrote, "I shall never be able to forget what I saw. People were struggling in the water, clustered so thickly that they literally covered the surface of the river. A few were swimming; the rest were floundering about, some clinging to a life raft that had floated free, others clutching at anything they could reach - at bits of wood, at each other, grabbing each other, pulling each other down, and screaming! The screaming was the most horrible of all. They were already pulling them out from below when I got there, out of the water and out through the portholes. People were being dragged out, wet, bleeding, and hysterical, by the scores. Most of those from the decks and the inside of the boat were cut more or less severely, because the chairs and benches had slid down on top of them when the boat went over. Those who had no injuries beyond the wetting and the shock were sent to the various hotels."

In spite of her frightening surroundings, Repa put her training right to work. "I started working, first on the boat itself and then on the dock, helping to try and resuscitate those who were unconscious. The pulmotors had not yet arrived, and we had to try what "first aid" measures we could. The injured were taken over to the Iroquois Memorial Hospital. Remembering that this is only an emergency hospital, and is not equipped to handle a large number of cases at once, I asked a policeman how many nurses were on duty there. He said that there were only two. Knowing that I would be more needed there than at the dock, for the present, I hurried over. I went back and forth between the hospital and the dock several times during the day, and had no trouble in making the journey quickly. I simply jumped on a patrol wagon or an ambulance, and being, as I have said, in uniform, was able to make the trip without being questioned."

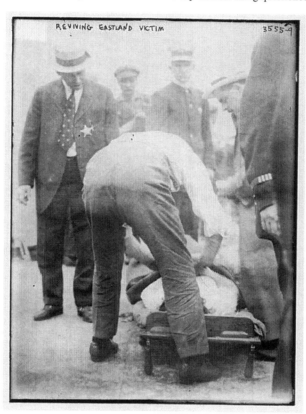

A picture of attempts to revive a victim

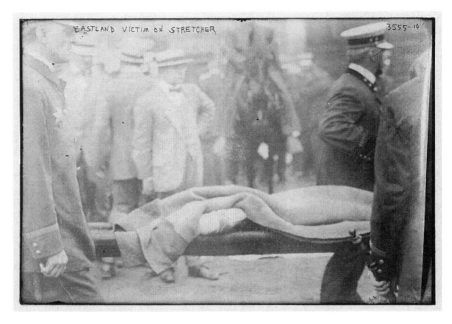

A picture of a victim on a stretcher

Unfortunately, the chaos of her surroundings often kept Repa from doing all that she wanted to. She later explained, "The one place I did have trouble, and a great deal of it, was at the dock. The police had evidently received orders to keep everybody back, and so zealously did they perform their work that I was held up several times until I could be identified. I finally remembered the arm bands that we nurses had received to wear at the picnic. These were of red, white and blue cloth, with a red cross on them. After I had put mine on I had no further trouble."

Things back at the hospital were nearly as desperate as conditions at the dock, but those in the area also rose to the challenge of helping others. Repa continued, "When I got to the Iroquois I found the two nurses distracted. More and more people were arriving every minute, wet and shivering, and there were no blankets left. Something had to be done quickly, so I had one of the nurses telephone to Marshall Field & Company for 500 blankets, with orders to charge them to the Western Electric Company. In the meantime I telephoned to some of the nearby restaurants and had them send over hot soup and coffee to the hospital. By this time the hospital was so full of people that we had no place to put the less seriously injured while they were drying off. Luckily, just at this time, word came from men working in the boiler room of a large building nearby that they would care for as many people as we cared to send over. I must say that the people of Chicago showed a wonderful spirit. Everyone did all he could to help. As soon as my patients were sufficiently recovered, I would send them home, thinking it better to have them with their families as soon as possible. In order to do this, I would simply go out into the street, stop the first automobile that came along, load it up with people, and tell the owner or driver where to take them. And not one driver said "no," or seemed anything but anxious to help out! When the women would be brought off the boat dripping wet, the men standing by simply took off their coats and put them around them."

As the search for the living gave way to a search for the dead, reporters were already quick to the scene. Even as the disaster was ongoing, Mrs. William Peterson told one of them, "I was pulled clear under water and when I came to the surface, I saw two hands reaching out of a porthole. They pulled me through. I don't know whether my husband, daughter and sister-in-law were saved or not."

Just when it seemed circumstances could not get any worse, the weather turned foul and further hampered what had now become more of a recovery operation than rescue efforts. Nurse Repa recalled, "About nine or half-past I started back to the dock. When I got to Clark Street the crowd was so dense that I simply couldn't walk a step further. So I got on a hook and ladder truck that was going down. When I got to the dock they had begun to bring the bodies up from the hold, and it was pouring rain. The bodies came out faster than we could handle them. By this time a number of outside nurses and doctors were at work on the victims. Most of them were dead, but a few still showed signs of life. I saw that if any of these were to be saved we must get them away from the dock. The crowding and confusion were terrible. The bodies were laid out on the dock, on the bridges, some on the Roosevelt, others on the sidewalk. A crowd of willing but ignorant volunteers kept getting in the way, and made our attempts at resuscitation almost useless. I asked one of the policemen: 'Isn't there some building where we can take these people? Some of them have a fighting chance if we can get them in out of the rain and away from this crowd.' He promised to see what could be done, and went away. A little later he returned, saying that we could take the bodies over to Reid & Murdoch's warehouse. We took the bodies we had, and all the others that came out, over there; but it was too late. Out of hundreds that we took to the warehouse, only four were revived."

As the day wore on, the chaos and desperation in the area only increased, and more and more family members rushed around searching for missing loved ones. Repa wrote, "By this time I had on my arm band, and so was able to go from the dock to the warehouse and back without being stopped. What made the confusion at the dock still worse was the fact that many of the people who had been pulled out of the water uninjured were still so dazed that they were wandering up and down without knowing where they were or what they were doing. I found one man up a little alley nearby. He was wandering up and down, with a ghastly, expressionless face, repeating over and over again, "I lost them all, I lost them all." His wife and three children were somewhere in the hold of the Eastland. About twelve o'clock they reached the bodies in the inner cabins; and after that time all the bodies that came up seemed to be women and children. It had begun to drizzle just before the boat was to start, and the mothers had taken their children inside to be out of the wet. In the meantime my sister was looking for me in the morgues and at Reid & Murdoch's. Someone had telephoned to my home that I had been seen climbing over the side of the boat and had fallen off. I was working over a man down at the warehouse when I heard someone scream, 'My God, it's Helen!' It was my sister. She fainted when she saw me."

Finally it was obvious that there was little else to be accomplished. Repa concluded her harrowing tale: "When I started out in the morning I had had on a white uniform and white shoes. By noon, what with dressing wounds and kneeling on the dock, I was covered with bloodstains and caked with mud from head to foot. I had lost my coat. A fireman threw a woman's skirt over my shoulders, and I kept the rain out with that. At four o'clock I went home. There was nothing left to do. I had been on my feet since seven-thirty that morning, and I felt that if I ever sat down I would never get up again. I came home in the street car, with the skirt wrapped around my shoulders and my brother's raincoat over that."

Pictures of victims being pulled from the wreck

A picture of a building full of victims

In the midst of the larger tragedy was a smaller one, as the *Chicago Daily Tribune* reported on a little boy who no one came to claim: "'Whose little boy is that?' Almost every one seeking relatives or friends at the Second Regiment armory morgue has asked the question as they passed the body of a dark, curly haired boy, between 8 and 9 years old. Some mothers, looking for their own babies, have shed their tears over him as they gazed at the little face. Sadly they have shaken their heads and asked the question. The body, numbered 396, has been there since 4 o'clock Saturday afternoon. The boy had been dressed all in white."

Eventually, the boy was finally identified. The paper reported, "THIS LITTLE EASTLAND VICITM IS IDENTIFIED AT LAST. Two boys yesterday identified body No 396 as Willie Novotny, their 7 year old playmate." When 13,000 people from the city showed up to bury him, Mayor Big Bill Thompson said movingly, "The hearts of all Chicagoans go out in grief to the sufferers from this calamity. The city mourns."

Chapter 6: Strong Evidence

"The federal prosecutors had very strong evidence. More than eight hundred deaths, a steamship capsized while still tied to its dock. No act of God. No iceberg. No torpedo. Two chief engineers of the Eastland confessed to investigators in Chicago that the ship owners had discussed stability problems in 1914 and 1915. ... There was a history of near-accidents on the Eastland going back a dozen years. Surely, the owners were negligent if they didn't bother to learn about them. ... In front of the coroner's jury in Chicago, Steele— the self-proclaimed angel of the Eastland's company— lied repeatedly. As to the government's steamboat-inspection service, it simply didn't connect the dots as the Eastland moved from Lake Michigan to Lake Erie and then back. The inspectors themselves set off red flags, then failed to follow them up. In the next ten days, the captain would weep on the stand, and the two sides would clash over everything, even whether the Chicago River technically existed anymore. ... Now, seven months after the disaster, was the moment for justice. There was surely criminal misconduct with such a horrific number of wrongful deaths. The guilty would surely be exposed. Long penitentiary sentences were surely coming— unless the defense could somehow outduel the prosecutors." - Michael McCarthy, *Ashes Under Water: The SS Eastland and the Shipwreck That Shook America.*

A picture of the *Eastland* being righted after the disaster

Within days of the disaster, a coroner's jury was convened to hear the evidence about what went wrong with the *Eastland* and render an opinion about what, if anything, should be done. During the hearing, Greenbaum was questioned extensively on whether or not he felt the government inspections were sufficient for ensuring that the ships plying the Great Lakes were safe for passengers. He replied, "We have to apply for a certificate in the spring. The inspection certificate is given for one year's time. They come over and examine the boat, and if they find everything O. K., they give a certificate to operate for the year, and then they make occasional inspections to see that everything is in good order. ... The Government steamboat boiler inspector has to thoroughly examine and see that all mechanical apparatus aboard the steamer conforms with the Government rules and regulations. The Government — the boiler inspector, I presume, is the one that prepares the questions which the men have to answer when they get their license. I believe the boiler inspector and the hull inspector jointly sign the license. [The inspector] should be a man well versed in everything pertaining to it. He should have graduated from the ranks, started as a coal passer, fireman, gone up through as oiler, fireman, first, second and third assistant. ... A hull inspector — his mode of advancement would be to start as a seaman, as a lookout, wheelsman, on up to mate, then to captain. ... At the present time there are three certificates each...One given to the collector of customs, one is given to the boat, and it is retained in the office of the inspectors."

Greenbaum was also questioned about other inspections his company made to their vessels. He added, "We carry insurance on the boats and the insurance representatives at different intervals come down and inspect the steamers when we have the boats in the dry dock ; they always come there to see that everything is fit and proper. We put the boats in dock — dry dock — each spring, to be sure that everything is right. They always have men down there."

Since overcrowding was considered one of the contributing factors in the Eastland *incident*, the coroner's jury questioned Greenbaum about how ships were given information regarding the number of passengers they could carry. He told them, "The Government regulation provides for a certain number of passengers between the 15th of May and the 15th of October; in addition, it provides for a number after that period; then if you alter your boat at all during the year, put on additional equipment, you make an application to the inspector. There is not only inspectors, but the Government has a boat that goes around occasionally to see whether the requirements are being complied with in order with the Government. The other day, at the time of the disaster, we threw several hundred life preservers overboard; that decreased the equipment. Before letting the Roosevelt go out the next morning I called up the steamboat inspector, and asked him, and he reduced my capacity until we got repair for the equipment that was lost. ... I think their rules were changed — I think their rules now provide they must inspect two or three times during the season of operation. ...I have seen them numerous times. They are down around the docks every Sunday; I have seen them other times. We had a large party to handle on the 28th of June; they were down; they. were on the Roosevelt about two weeks ago; they went on at Michigan City and had a fire drill over there — made them put the boats over to see that the men were acquainted with operating the life-boats."

Next, the jury inquired about the training that those in charge of the ships received. Greenbaum assured them, "The captain and the engineer are required to see that their subordinates are — that they have their proper papers. As I recall, it is punishable by fine if they do not; then there is a space on the boat where the license must be exhibited for public inspection. We have three spaces for engineers and the same number for the captain and the mates. ... We presume the Government, in issuing a license, knows they are competent. In the selection of our men we determine their past record, their general reputation."

Greenbaum also discussed the method of loading the steamer: "In unloading passengers, the ballast, would be to take the water out, so that would bring the boat up and putting the passengers, to hold the boat stable. My idea would be to have the water in her. I supposed the water was in it on the outer. My idea was that the water — my idea was that they were to hold the water over on the left side, so as to raise the gangway to make it easier of access to the passengers to come aboard. ...the tendency of the people when they go aboard is to stay on the side where their friends are coming down the dock, so that would take the water on the outside, so the reason to trim the tank so as to offset the weight on that side."

Finally, Greenbaum had to provide an answer for why the *Eastland* capsized, and while he conceded he could give no definitive answer, he did speculate on a couple of possibilities: "Why, one would have been the matter of having the ballast in her hull properly, I believe if the boat had been filled with water, she wouldn't have gone over, and other one would have been the question of having too much water on one side, and another would have been if the boat listed over, the portholes down in the hull might have been closed and the water gone in, and another one would have been the question of a great deal of weight, that is, the body of the people going over on one side, and another one would have been, but this didn't happen, because the tug hadn't started to pull her out."

As a result of this and other testimony, the grand jury issued indictments for manslaughter against the president of the steamship company and three other officers associated with the company. It also indicted Captain Pedersen and his engineer for criminal carelessness.

A picture of Captain Pedersen

Ultimately, the men were never brought to trial after a court found "barely a scintilla of proof" with which to proceed. Instead, those who lost loved ones in the disaster had to be satisfied with the comfort that could only come from time. Meanwhile, the world moved on, mostly engulfed in the war then spreading across Europe. In fact, the *Eastland* would eventually be salvaged and converted into the USS *Wilmette*, a naval gunboat, and when the papers began to carry stories of thousands killed in a single battle, the 800+ folks who died that day in Chicago all too quickly faded from memory.

A picture of the USS *Wilmette*

A marker commemorating the *Eastland*

Bibliography

Bonansinga, Jay. *The Sinking of the Eastland: America's Forgotten Tragedy*, Citadel Press 2004.

Hilton, George. *Eastland: Legacy of the Titanic*, Stanford University Press 1997.

McCarthy, Michael. *Ashes Under Water: The SS Eastland and the Shipwreck that Shook America*, Lyons Press 2014.

Wachholz, Ted. *The Eastland Disaster*, Arcadia Publishing 2005.

Online Resources

Other books about famous shipwrecks by Charles River Editors

The Sinking of the Edmund Fitzgerald: The Loss of the Largest Ship on the Great Lakes by Charles River Editors

Other titles about the General Slocum on Amazon

Video footage of the *Eastland* disaster can be found online at http://www.chicagotribune.com/news/daywatch/chi-eastland-disaster-film-footage-20150208-htmlstory.html

Made in the USA
Middletown, DE
21 August 2019